COOKING IN BOXERS

with

CHEF BAILEY

50 Ways To Keep Your Mate In Bed

Mark Anthony Bailey

Chef Bailey LLC
375 West 127th Street, Suite 1
New York, NY 10027
www.chefbailey.com

Chef Bailey LLC book titles may be purchased for business or promotional use or for special sales. For more information, please contact publisher at address above.

First Printing, 2018
ISBN: 978-0-692-89759-1
Library of Congress Control Number: 2017909778

Cover Photography: Kawai Matthews
Cover Design: Daniel Roedler
Inside/Back Cover Portraits: Syed Yaqeen
Food Styling and Photography: Mark Anthony Bailey
Layout Design and Typesetting: Daniel Roedler
Editor: Christina Faison
Copy Editor: Chauncey Bellamy

"Dining with one's friends and beloved family is certainly one of life's primal and most innocent delights, one that is both soul-satisfying and eternal."

– Julia Child

This book is dedicated to my father, **Jonathan David Bailey**, and my sister, **Geraldine Sophia Bailey.**

INGREDIENTS

ACKNOWLDEGEMENTS

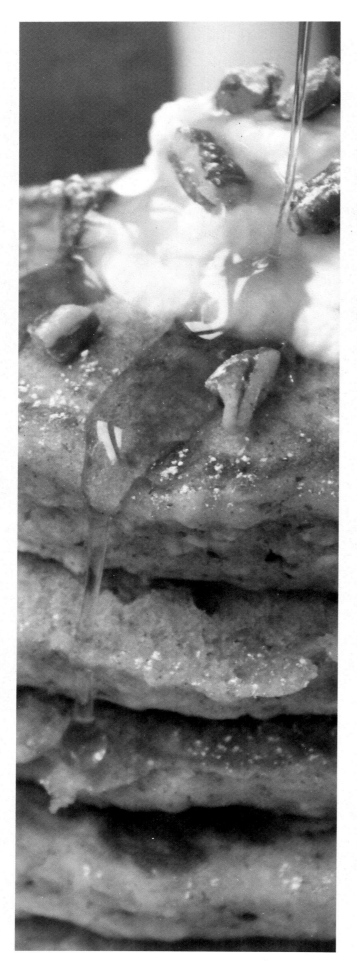

Thank you **God** for blessing me with this amazing journey to publish this cookbook. I prayed, and You answered.

Thank you **Mom** for being the best mother a son could ask for. Your unconditional love and support has made me the man I am today. I love you more than words can say.

I would like to extend a very special thanks to **Terrell Mullin**. You helped me launch my career as a chef, and if not for your expertise, support, and guidance, Chef Bailey would not be here today. Thank you for some of the most memorable times of my life. I owe you a big tray of macaroni and cheese!

To my very first client, **Niecy Nash**, thank you for your generosity and kindness and for taking a chance with an unknown (beginning) chef.

To **Eva Marcille**, thank you for your support and for inviting me into your home. You have proven that "Top Models" can be just as beautiful on the inside as they are on the outside. I owe you a jerk turkey!

Everyone has that special BFF with whom you share all of your dreams. For me, **Tarsha Vega** has been that friend. Thank you for listening to me talk about this cookbook and journey from its inception. Your support has been unwavering.

To **Shamara Ray**, thank you for being one of my closest confidants along this journey and for believing in me at times when I didn't believe in myself. Your support has been nothing shy of a blessing. Thank you for the advice, accountability, and great laughs along the way.

"Big Up" to **Neil Silvera**. Your friendship and support have been unchanging over the years. Thank you for your love and support.

"Shout out" to **Melissa "Missy" Mickens**. Thank you for being a real friend and one of my biggest cheerleaders.

To my closest foodie friends, **Tarin L. Rivera** and **Irene Perello**, thank you for being my greatest source of encouragement. You both have given me a lifetime of love, friendship, and support.

To **Carmen Aviles** and **Gina Perez**, thank you for the years of love, support, and Puerto Rican cuisine and for teaching me how to make a delicious Coquito!

To **Cindi Avila**, the best publicist and friend anyone with a dream can ask for. Thank you for taking a chance on this inexperienced chef with a big dream and a smile. You rock!

And I would be remiss not to thank the woman who gave me my very first break at a live television food segment, **Veronica Rosario**. You are an angel!

To **Christina Faison**, for whom I have just three words: The Best Editor! Thank you for helping me find my voice for this cookbook.

To my social media friends and fellow foodie followers, thank you for your online support. I appreciate every like, share, and comment!

Lastly, we all know it takes a village. Here is my village, whom all in their unique and special ways have inspired and ultimately made this cookbook possible. Thank you, **Village**!

Shawn Allen
Fay Armstrong
Gloria Armstrong
Donovan and Susy Bailey
Stafford Bailey
Jahmar Depass
Tarnisha Depass
Beverly Escofrey
Corine Hall
Latoya Hinds
Stephanie Hinds
Barbara King
Keisha Lewis
Wayne Stewart
Tamika Talbot
Angela Whyte
Taya Whyte
Li and Arlene Dolphy-Wong
William 'Grandpa' Alers
Ethan Owen Martinez
Jennifer Toro-Nealon and Pablo Nealon
Connie Ortiz
Lauren Ortiz and Richard Collazo
Elisabeth 'Libby' Rivera
The Perellos: Marcos, Isabelle, Gabe, and Georgia
Anthony and Dora Petsoulakis
Donnell and Courtney Arrington

Andre Beard
Danielle Bonner
Alexander Brown
Thomas Brown
Gordon Chambers
Sharon R. Chancie
Michael Embrey
Rich Gore
Kevin Harry
Chris and Lezli Harvell
Edgar Lantigua
Denise Lopez
Nancy Maisonette
Kawai Matthews
Winston Passley
Shanaya Reyes
Vanessa Richardson
Camile Sardina
A. Jade Smith
Dominique Williams
Melba Wilson
Fred Veasley and Yvonne Vega
Kristina Elena Vega

FOREWORD

I was so flattered when Mark asked me to write the foreword for this cookbook, especially when he said I would get a tray of his amazing Mac & Cheese (LOL). I am a professional makeup artist by vocation and a home chef by avocation, so I was instantly intrigued when Mark told me about his first cookbook, **Cooking in Boxers with Chef Bailey: 50 Ways to Keep Your Mate in Bed.**

In *Cooking in Boxers*, Mark offers over 50 excitingly unique as well as original breakfast recipes. Mark's eclectic cookery collection is comprised of all sorts of culinary erotica, yet the simple recipes could have you feeling like your very own Top Chef.

Looking through this cookbook, you will realize that it is so much more than just a collection of recipes. It offers insight into the warmth of the kitchen, providing tips and tools on how to keep the flame going with simple breakfast-in-bed gestures. It's also a practical cookbook, written by an expert who understands both his craft and how to explain it. With its important building blocks and basic techniques that are described step-by-step with many illustrations, this cookbook is definitely one of my absolute favorites.

Cooking In Boxers will be a very important part of your kitchen library. It's seriously fun, and it will nudge you to set aside your preconceptions about cookbooks. I wish all who try these recipes the lasting pleasure of an amazing breakfast in bed.

–Terrell Mullin, Celebrity Makeup Artist

INTRODUCTION

If breakfast is, in fact, the most important meal of the day, one might say breakfast in bed is the most important gesture a mate can make for his or her special someone. It is my belief that breakfast in bed is an expression of love like no other.

Quenching Potential Love Droughts

Let's face it: life can be very busy. Family, careers, children, chores, and life, in general, can sometimes cause us to put love on the back burner, dampening the chance to schedule those ever-eluding date nights and romantic dinners we long for and need. Fortunately, breakfast in bed offers a delicious alternative, as you'll be able to start the day with love rather than attempting to fit it in at the tail end of a busy schedule. Plus, breakfast in bed is really quite simple to plan.

First, it starts with the desire to show how much we care about our mates by choosing breakfast in bed as our love gesture. We, then, decide to go the extra mile by personally preparing this delicious meal. Next, we do some tasty, yet seductive, brainstorming on what to prepare, which will require some careful, romantic thought. Now comes the labor of love as we set out to prep, cook, and serve a breakfast that will not only heighten our mates' love, but also keep them in bed wanting seconds. Mission accomplished!

Blame it on Jamaica

So, why write a breakfast-in-bed cookbook? Besides being a hopeless romantic, I just love breakfast. It's been my favorite meal of the day for as long as I can remember. In fact, I can recall making my first breakfast at 8 years old, which consisted of cheesy scrambled eggs, sautéed Vienna sausages, and a buttery toasted bagel.

This first attempt at breakfast would have this young, budding chef in love with breakfast for a lifetime. However, while I enjoyed whipping up my own breakfast, I favored a good ole fashioned Jamaican breakfast prepared at the hands of my mom far more.

Being born in the Bronx to Jamaican parents certainly had its culinary advantages. Being raised by a family of cooks in a culture that takes great pride in its food and cooking was priceless. Sundays, a huge day of cooking in almost all Jamaican households, would find my mother in the kitchen cooking breakfast early in the morning. This meant waking up to the scent of sautéing peppers, scallions, garlic, and other mouth-watering aromas that a delicious Jamaican breakfast has to offer.

Food is Love

While my organic love of breakfast serves as inspiration for this cookbook, I would be remiss not to acknowledge that I believe in the simple motto, food is love. When done correctly and from the heart, it can speak volumes to our loved ones. But what kind of love are we talking about here? The love that connects us comes in many forms. As you will learn in this cookbook, food also has an obvious connection to romance, seduction, and, ultimately, making whoopee.

Food and Love

Yes, there is an obvious connection between food and love. The intense feeling of deep affection we feel for our mates can only be matched by our deep affinity for all things food. After all, it has been said that there is nothing we humans crave more than food and companionship. It seems that both food and love feed our souls and leave us comforted.

This sense of comfort is why I've included some popular comfort-food recipes of the South in the *Southern Comforts* chapter of this book. "Stick to your ribs" recipes, like **Sausage Biscuits and Gravy**, **Bacon-Wrapped Jerk Shrimp & Grits**, and **Fried Jerk Chicken and Waffles**, guarantee to keep your mate in bed. Alternatively, do a little teasing with recipes from my *Tease the Season* chapter that features breakfast recipes for holidays and seasons. Christmas, Valentine's Day, and pumpkin season are all celebrated in this chapter, where you will find timely breakfast recipes like **Pumpkin Oat Pancakes** and **Bacon-Wrapped Stuffin' Muffins**.

Food and Romance

One of the many powers of food is its divine ability to romance us. Think about it: when garnished with edibles, any backdrop can be easily transformed into the most romantic of settings. For a romantic breakfast in bed, I've included recipes that can best romanticize the whole experience. In *Home Cooking*, a chapter where I share Jamaican-inspired breakfast recipes, you will find the national dish of the island, ackee and saltfish, entitled **Ackee and Codfish Sauté**. Try romancing your mate's palate with this rousing yet mystifying dish. Or, if planning a romantic breakfast for dinner, try any of the recipes in the *Breakfast After Dark* chapter. They're sure to keep the spark going from night to morning.

Food and Seduction

I avidly believe that we eat with our eyes. Round in shape, yellow in color, drizzled, or melted are all ways that food appeals to the eye. This works in our favor as we aim to seduce our mate with our breakfast-in-bed visual favorites. *Eye Candy* is a chapter comprised of eye-catching Eggs Benedict recipes that will flirt with your mate's sense of vision. You can even lure your mate in with the scent of bacon with any number of recipes in the *Bacon Lovers* chapter. No matter what recipe your mate votes for, the eyes have it.

Food is a Science, but I'm Not a Scientist

Science credits aphrodisiacs, food that stimulates our frisky desires, for the link between food and lovemaking. Certain foods such as oysters, chocolate, and chili peppers have long been touted as our biggest aphrodisiacs. However, did you know that blueberries, pumpkin spice, and basil are also capable of getting our juices flowing? Yes, it seems that aphrodisiacs can be found in a host of ingredients, many used for recipes in this very cookbook. Having a knowledge of the effects that certain foods will have on your mate's libido can prove beneficial when crafting the ideal breakfast in bed. Instead of going only with the obvious, I included a host of ingredients not commonly known as aphrodisiacs.

Spirits have long been thought of as aphrodisiacs in a glass. Because having a drink to get us in the mood is more common than not, try doing a little bartending for breakfast with any of my breakfast cocktail recipes in the *Drunk in Love* chapter.

Fruits like bananas, berries, and even avocados are also aphrodisiacs that I've incorporated in my recipes. Whether by chemical makeup, fragrance, or shape, these fruits are all known aphrodisiacs, making them ideal for breakfast in bed. My low-calorie recipes in the *Skinny Breakfast* chapter and my sweet syrup-based recipes in the *Sweet Hearts* chapter are great recipes that feature some of these lusty little fruits.

It should go without saying that I am in no way a scientist. I do not hold a physician's degree, nor am I trained to diagnose. I am what I call myself, a doctor of love, and my prescription to kick it up a notch in the bedroom is to try brunching in the sack. It's a surefire way to feed your mate's appetite not only for food, but also for love.

In this cookbook, you will find a host of recipes that further validates the notion that food is an expression of love. Learn just how much when you express your love with any of these 50 recipes that will undoubtedly keep your mate in bed wanting more.

Welcome to **Cooking in Boxers with Chef Bailey: 50 Ways to Keep Your Mate in Bed!**

DRUNK IN LOVE

"Drink her love, like your favorite liquor."

– Richard Matthews

We've all been there: drunk in love on a deliciously romantic date. We typically start the night with our favorite cocktail. (And why not? We're all responsible adults who sometimes need a little love-in-a-bottle to get us in the mood.) Next, we nibble on shared appetizers, which only fuel the fire. Along with that second cocktail comes some "innocent" flirting that leads us to trade words for action on the dance floor. Before you know it (uh oh!), last call gives way to an intoxicating night or perhaps a morning of passion.

What is this connection between libations and love? And why, when under the influence of both, can we seemingly not get enough of our mate? Well, research shows that women and men who drink modestly have higher levels of desire than do those who drink less. As it turns out, our "date starter," poured in a glass, is actually an aphrodisiac. Therefore, no breakfast in bed is complete without a cocktail. It's the perfect "hot" shot to get those love juices flowing first thing in the morning.

I've got four morning love potions that I like to whip up when serving breakfast in bed. For champagne lovers, try my **Straw-Bailey Bliss**, which is a fun strawberry twist on your basic mimosa. If your mate needs that morning java pick-me-up, he or she will love my lusciously spiked iced coffee, **Love Hangover**. Lovers of morning citrus juices will enjoy my citrus sangria, **Spanish Fly**, which combines pineapple juice and an orange-flavored liqueur with white wine. And finally, for the ultimate romantic morning fling, try my chocolate martini with a grenadine twist, otherwise known as **Red Bottoms**. This, of course, is best teased with **Chocolate-Covered Strawberries**.

STRAW-BAILEY BLISS

serves 2 | prep time: 10 minutes | cook time: 5 minutes

Ingredients

4 frozen strawberries
3oz. gin
¼ tsp. sugar
champagne, chilled
2 fresh strawberries for garnish

Directions

Place 2 champagne flutes in a freezer, and chill for 10 minutes.

Meanwhile, combine the frozen strawberries, gin, and sugar in a blender. Blend until pureed. Spoon 1-2 teaspoons of the strawberry puree into the bottom of each flute. Top with champagne. Garnish each flute with a strawberry slice.

Serve chilled.

This twist to the classic mimosa pairs the fruit of love with the bubbly of love. Champagne and strawberry make for a blissful morning when served with breakfast in bed.

Women love chocolate, but do they love Red Bottoms more? Fortunately, with my chocolate martini over chilled grenadine–also known as Red Bottoms–your mate won't have to choose.

RED BOTTOMS

serves 2 | prep time: 15 minutes | cook time: 5 minutes

Ingredients

1oz. grenadine or cherry liquor
1½oz. chocolate liqueur
3oz. vodka
3oz. Bailey's Irish Cream

Directions

Gather 2 martini glasses. Pour half of an ounce of grenadine in each glass. Transfer to the freezer, and chill for 15 minutes or until the grenadine hardens.

Meanwhile, combine 4-5 ice cubes with the chocolate liqueur, vodka, and Bailey's in a martini shaker. Cover and shake for 1-2 minutes.

Remove the chilled glasses of grenadine from the freezer, and gently top each glass with the chocolate martini mixture making sure to strain out the ice cubes.

This drink is best served chilled and alongside *Chocolate-Covered Strawberries*.

CHOCOLATE-COVERED STRAWBERRIES

1 cup semi-sweet dark chocolate morsels
2 tbsp. heavy cream
1lb. fresh strawberries

Line a baking sheet with wax paper. Set aside. Rinse and dry the strawberries.

Fill a medium saucepan with water 1-2 inches deep. Bring to a boil over medium-high heat. Reduce the heat to medium-low. Add the chocolate morsels and cream to a medium glass mixing bowl. Place the bowl over the saucepan. Stir the morsels and cream until the chocolate is melted smooth. Dip a strawberry into the melted chocolate, and transfer to the baking sheet. Repeat with the remaining strawberries. Chill them in the refrigerator until the chocolate sets.

Serve chilled.

SPANISH FLY

serves 4 | prep time: 20 minutes

The Spanish really know a thing or two about love potions. Spain, the country responsible for sangria, traditionally uses red wine, chopped fruit, and orange juice or brandy to create that love punch. For my *Spanish Fly*, I've paired white wine with pineapple juice and orange-flavored liqueur, making this an important love agent for that romantic breakfast in the sack.

Ingredients

1 bottle white wine (sauvignon blanc or citrusy wine)
¾ cup orange-flavored liqueur
2 cups club soda
½ cup simple syrup, chilled
2 cups pineapple juice
1 cup pineapple chunks, frozen
½ cup blueberries, frozen

Directions

In a large pitcher, combine all ingredients. Serve over ice.

LOVE HANGOVER

serves 4 | prep time: 25 minutes

For many, liquid caffeine—also known as coffee—is the only beverage of choice first thing in the morning, especially when trying to nurse a hangover. However, that's not all coffee can do. Turns out coffee increases our blood flow, perking up our body parts, which can, in turn, give us an energy rush that can surely enhance our bedroom activities. I'll certainly drink to that.

Love Hangover, my spiked iced coffee cocktail, is a great caffeinated quick-pick-me-up made with rich roasted coffee, milk, and a dark spirit.

Ingredients

4 tbsp. ground coffee
3 cups iced water
3 tbsp. condensed milk
1 tbsp. half-and-half
¼ tsp. vanilla extract
4-5 ice cubes
2 tsp. dark spirit (dark rum, bourbon, etc.)
whipped cream topping
cocoa powder, for dusting

Directions

Place 2 glass coffee mugs in the freezer to chill.

Meanwhile, combine the water and coffee in a 4-cup French press. Using a spoon, mix the coffee and water until well combined (approximately 1 minute). Cover with the lid, but do not press the plunger. Allow the mixture to steep for 5 minutes.

Press the plunger through the coffee mixture until it reaches the bottom. Pour the coffee mixture into a 4-cup or larger mason jar or container with a lid. Add the ice cubes, condensed milk, half-and-half, and vanilla extract. Cover the jar and shake the coffee vigorously until well combined, about 2 minutes. Set aside.

Remove the coffee mugs from the freezer, and pour 1 teaspoon of your dark spirit of choice into each mug. Strain the iced coffee into each mug. Top the coffee with whipped cream, and dust with cocoa powder.

Serve chilled.

HOME COOKING

"When the root is strong, the fruit is sweet."

-Bob Marley

Being born to Jamaican parents has had more than just a major impact on my cooking style: after a recent trip to Jamaica for "recreational research," I learned of its additional influence on my passion for cooking for love. That visit was my first as a chef, and I was very eager to take in the Caribbean's most romantic destination with a culinary eye.

Passionate is probably the best word to describe Jamaicans, and this very passion extends from their cooking to romance. It is said that, "Jamaicans bring the spice to the kitchen and the bedroom." This "spice" is all around them. So, how could I not notice the egg-shaped clouds decorating the crisp blue skies, the long stretches of sugary white beaches ebbing the salty ocean, or the sweet tropical fruit hanging low in its ripeness while the fertile ground yields yams, potatoes, and cassava? Jamaica by definition is an amorous oasis—and a true foodie's paradise.

Sundays are the most important days of cooking in Jamaica. Fragrant scallions, garlic, and peppers are common aromas one wakes up to on a Sunday morning. While popular breakfast staples—like eggs, bacon, and toast—are common, a typical island breakfast tends to be a little bit heartier. Ackee and Codfish, Brown Stew Liver, Callaloo with Salted Mackerel are just a few of the island's hearty breakfast dishes. Fried dumplings, also known as Jamaican fried biscuits, are almost always served, making them perfect for sopping up all that flavorful sauce. And of course, who can forget Jamaica's popular breakfast in a bowl known as porridge?

The following recipes in this chapter are some of my favorite Jamaican breakfast dishes. They are simple, hearty, flavorful, and a true representation of my cooking roots and inspiration. If you and your mate have yet to visit this romantic isle, then you should bring "the spice" of the island to your bedroom with any of these Jamaican-inspired recipes.

Did you know that vanilla, when consumed, can be a sexual stimulant in both women and men? My Jamaican plantain porridge, made with pure vanilla beans, guarantees some warm and snuggly moments to follow.

PLANTAIN PORRIDGE

serves 2 | prep time: 23 minutes | cook time: 1 hour

Ingredients

1 green banana, peeled and cut into 1-2" slices
1 yellow plantain, peeled and cut into 1-2" slices
4 cups water
13½oz. can coconut milk
1 tsp. cinnamon powder
½ cup brown sugar
2 vanilla beans, split lengthwise
¼ tsp. nutmeg
dash of salt
8-10 water crackers (optional)

Directions

Combine the water, green banana, and plantain in a blender. Puree until smooth. If chunky after blending, strain the liquid by discarding the plantain bits.

Transfer the mixture to a medium pot over medium-low heat. Cook while stirring for approximately 15 minutes to prevent lumping. Once thickened, stir in the milk, salt, cinnamon, sugar, nutmeg, and vanilla beans. Reduce the heat to low, and simmer for approximately 45 minutes, stirring occasionally.

Serve warm with 4-5 water crackers.

CORNMEAL PORRIDGE

serves 2 | prep time: 10 minutes | cook time: 20 minutes

Ingredients

4 cups water
1 cup whole milk
2 cinnamon sticks
2 vanilla beans, split lengthwise
1 cup yellow cornmeal
½ cup sweetened condensed milk (or light brown sugar)
dash of salt
nutmeg for garnish
8-10 water crackers (optional)

Directions

In a medium saucepan, combine 3 cups of water with the whole milk, cinnamon sticks, vanilla bean stems, and salt. Cover and bring to a boil over medium-high heat.

In a medium bowl, whisk together the cornmeal and the remaining cup of water. Stir until the mixture forms a pasty batter.

When the mixture in the saucepan begins to boil, stir in the cornmeal mixture. Reduce the heat to low, and continue stirring to prevent lumping. Sweeten with the condensed milk to taste. If the porridge is too thick, add a quarter cup of milk, and stir for 3-5 minutes while cooking. Remove the vanilla bean stems, and discard.

Remove the porridge from the heat. Serve warm, in a bowl, with a dash of nutmeg and 4-5 water crackers.

Because nothing affects our emotions more than the weather, try whipping up this bowl of golden comfort on a wintry morning. This cornmeal porridge, served with crackers, will keep your breakfast in bed warm and cozy.

Interactive food, food that requires the use of hands for eating and dipping, is ideal for breakfast in bed. These fritters are a great hands-on breakfast starter to get your taste buds in the mood.

CODFISH FRITTERS

serves 2 | prep time: 15 minutes | cook time: 20 minutes

Ingredients

8 cups water
1 lb. boneless salted cod fillet
2 cups self-rising flour
1 tbsp. baking powder
1 tbsp black pepper
2 tsp. Old Bay seasoning
2 tsp. dried thyme
¾ cup scallions, chopped
1 tsp. pepper sauce
3 tbsp. ketchup
2-3 cups vegetable oil, for frying

Directions

In a large pot, bring 8 cups of water to a boil over high heat. Add the salted codfish to the water, and boil for 1 hour to reduce the salt. Add additional water as it reduces.

Meanwhile, in a medium bowl, combine the flour, baking powder, black pepper, Old Bay seasoning, and thyme. Mix well. Stir in 1 cup of water and the pepper sauce. Stir the mixture into a thick and pasty batter.

Strain the fish, and transfer it to a small bowl. Using a fork, break the fish into small pieces. Fold the fish, followed by the scallions and ketchup, into the batter. Stir until combined. Set aside for 10-15 minutes to allow the batter to set.

Heat the oil in a deep fryer or skillet to 350° F. Working in batches, drop spoonfuls (approximately a quarter cup) of batter into the oil. Fry the fritter for 2-3 minutes or until golden brown. If frying in a skillet, fry for approximately 2 minutes per side until golden brown.

Remove the fritters, and transfer them to a platter lined with a paper towel to drain any excess oil.

Serve warm with **Lemon-Dill Cream Sauce**.

LEMON-DILL CREAM SAUCE

½ cup sour cream
½ cup mayonnaise
1 tbsp. fresh dill, minced
1 tbsp. lemon zest
juice of 1 lemon
salt and pepper to taste

Combine the sour cream, mayonnaise, dill, zest, lemon juice in a medium bowl. Mix well. Add salt and black pepper to taste.

ACKEE & CODFISH

serves 4 | prep time: 15 minutes | cook time: 1 hour, 20 minutes

Ask a native Jamaican what a typical dish served for breakfast on the island is, and more than likely, the first response will be ackee and saltfish. After all, ackee—a pear-shaped fruit with a buttery and nutty flavor—that has been picked over, boiled, and sautéed with seasoned codfish is the national dish of the country.

Do you want that hands-on experience? Try srving this dish with fried dumplings to sop up all that delicious juice.

Ingredients

6-8 cups water
1 lb. boneless salted cod fillet
½ cup vegetable oil, divided into ¼ cups
2 strips bacon, chopped
1 medium onion, diced
4 garlic cloves, chopped
1 bell pepper, diced
2 small tomatoes, diced
3 scallion stalks, diced green stem only
1 scotch bonnet pepper, seeded and diced (optional)
1 sprig thyme
1 tbsp. black pepper
1 tbsp. Old Bay seasoning
20oz. can ackee

Directions

In a large pot, bring the water and the salted codfish to a boil over high heat. Boil for 1 hour to reduce the salt. Add additional water as it reduces. Strain the fish from the water, and shred it. Set aside.

In a large skillet, heat a quarter cup of oil over medium-high. Add the bacon, onion, and garlic, and sauté for 2-3 minutes until the ingredients become fragrant. Stir in the bell pepper, and continue to sauté for an additional 2 minutes. Stir in the cod, tomato, scallion, Scotch bonnet pepper, thyme, black pepper, Old Bay, and remaining oil. Mix well. Cover the skillet, reduce the heat to medium-low, and simmer for 10-12 minutes.

Gently fold the ackee into the sautéed fish. Be careful not to overstir to prevent the ackee from becoming mushy. Simmer for 5 minutes or until heated through.

Serve warm with **Fried Dumplings** (p. 38).

SPINACH & CODFISH

serves 4
prep time: 1 hour
cook time: 20 minutes

Ingredients

6-8 cups water
1 lb. boneless salted cod fillet
½ cup olive oil, divided in ¼ cups
1 large onion, peeled and sliced
2 garlic cloves, minced
1 tbsp. ground black pepper
3 cups fresh baby spinach or kale

Directions

In a large pot, bring the water and the salted codfish to a boil over high heat. Boil for 1 hour to reduce the salt. Add additional water as it reduces. Strain the fish from the water, and shred it. Set aside.

In a large skillet, heat a quarter cup of olive oil over medium-high. Add the onion and garlic, and sauté until fragrant. Add the fish to the skillet, and season it with black pepper. Cook while stirring for 5-7 minutes. Add the spinach and the remaining oil. Mix well. Reduce the heat to medium-low, and cover. Allow the fish-and-spinach sauté to cook for 5-10 minutes or until heated through.

Serve warm with *Fried Dumplings*.

FRIED DUMPLINGS

prep time: 40 minutes
cook time: 15 minutes

2 cups all-purpose flour
2 tsp. baking powder
1 tsp. salt
1 tbsp. sugar
½ cup butter, diced
½ cup warm water
1 cup vegetable oil

In a large bowl, combine the flour, baking powder, salt, sugar, and butter. Mix well. Slowly stir in the water, kneading the flour mixture into dough. If the dough is too sticky, add 1-2 tablespoons of flour.

On a floured surface, roll out the dough. For approximately 5 minutes, knead until the dough is smooth. Return the dough to the bowl, and cover it to allow it to rise. Set aside for 30 minutes.

To form the dumplings, break off a piece of the dough about the size of a golf ball, and shape it into a round dumpling patty. Repeat with the remaining dough.

In a skillet, heat the oil over high heat. Reduce the heat to medium-high, and add the dumplings one at a time. Fry the dumplings for approximately 2 minutes per side until lightly browned. Transfer the dumplings to a paper towel to drain any excess oil, and cool. Serve warm.

Very similar to the national dish of Jamaica, this recipe offers up an equally tasty alternative to ackee when substituted with spinach, callaloo or kale.

SKINNY BREAKFAST

"Diets, like clothes, should be tailored to you."

-Joan Rivers

Food is an event that should be celebrated at all times; yes, even while on a diet. With millions of Americans dieting each year, chances are you and your mate may be doing a little weight-watching of your own.

This chapter offers an alternative breakfast-in-bed experience for those who may be counting calories. Egg recipes, like my **Baked Egg Avocado with Mango Salsa** and **Spicy Tomato and Turkey Sausage Egg Bakes**, keep these dishes light, high in protein, low in calories, and most importantly, tasty! For a slightly heartier breakfast, try my **Quinoa Breakfast Bowl**, which is rich in fiber and protein. And this chapter would not be complete without my deliciously nutritious **Banana-Berry Avocado Smoothie**.

Remember, a couple that diets together works out together, so be ready for some marathon sessions after serving up any one of these energy-fueled recipes.

BANANA-BERRY AVOCADO SMOOTHIE

serves 2 | prep time: 10 minutes

Did you know that some scientists say that blueberries are known as the natural Viagra? Turns out that little blueberries may have something in common with those little blue pills. Blueberries can cause the body's blood vessels to relax, which, in turn, enhances blood circulation, helping blood to flow to all of those important body parts.

Skip the little blue pill, and make your mate this stimulating smoothie, packed with three powerhouse fruits: banana, blueberry, and, yes, avocado.

Ingredients

2 ripe bananas, peeled and quartered
¾ cup fresh blueberries
2 cups fat-free milk (or substitute with almond milk or coconut water)
½ haas avocado, mashed
2 tbsp. honey or agave
¼ tsp. ground cinnamon
8-12 ice cubes
crushed almonds, for garnish

Directions

In a blender, combine the bananas, blueberries, and milk. Puree for 1-2 minutes. Add the avocado, honey, cinnamon, and 8-10 ice cubes. (For a frothier smoothie, add 2-3 more cubes.) Continue to blend until smooth.

Serve in a frozen mug or glass.

Top with banana slices or crushed nuts, if desired.

Another healthy ingredient that enhances blood circulation is the avocado. This pear-shaped produce is rich in unsaturated fat and low in saturated fat, making it a heart-healthy food to help you gear up for those romantic morning seconds and thirds.

Baked with an egg and topped with Mango Salsa, these avocados make for a light and healthy breakfast in bed.

BAKED EGG AVOCADO

serves 2 | prep time: 5 minutes | cook time: 15 minutes

Ingredients

2 hass avocados
4 medium eggs
1 tsp. Hungarian sweet paprika, separated
dash of salt

Directions

Preheat the oven to 350° F.

Using a long knife, cut the avocado in half by slicing evenly around the seed. Gently separate both halves, and remove the seed. Repeat with the second avocado to create 4 halves with small seed cavities for the eggs. To make the cavities slightly wider to hold the eggs, use a spoon to gently scoop around the edges of the cavity. Season each cavity with a dash of salt and about a quarter teaspoon of paprika.

Crack an egg in a small bowl. Using a spoon, transfer the yolk to an avocado pocket, then spoon in some of the egg white to fill the pocket. Transfer the avocado half to a baking dish. Repeat this step with the remaining eggs and avocado halves, and transfer to the oven. Bake for 12-15 minutes or until the eggs set to desired taste.

Serve warm, topped with **Mango Salsa**.

MANGO SALSA

1 small tomato, seeded and diced
½ medium red onion, diced
1 jalapeño pepper, seeded and diced
1 medium mango, peeled, seeded and diced
1 small tomatillo, diced
2 garlic cloves, minced
½ cup cilantro, chopped
1 tbsp. lime juice
1 tsp. sugar
dash of salt

In a large mixing bowl, combine all ingredients. Mix well. Refrigerate for 15-30 minutes.

Serve chilled or at room temperature.

SPICY TOMATO & TURKEY SAUSAGE BAKED EGGS

serves 2 | prep time: 5 minutes | cook time: 25 minutes

Ingredients

1 tbsp. olive oil
2 turkey sausage links, chopped and casings removed
2 garlic cloves, minced
1 small onion, diced
2 tsp. ground black pepper
1 cup crushed tomatoes
¼ cup tomato paste
1 small chili pepper
1 tbsp. parsley, chopped
4 eggs
Melba toast (optional)

Directions

Preheat the oven to 350° F.

In a medium skillet, heat the oil over medium-high. Add the sausage, and sauté until cooked. Stir in the onion and garlic, then season with black pepper. Continue to sauté for 2-3 minutes or until fragrant. Stir in the crushed tomatoes, sauce, pepper, and parsley. Reduce the heat to medium-low, and simmer for 10 minutes. Remove from the heat.

Using a ladle, evenly spoon the sauce into 4 ramekins. Gently top each with an egg, careful not to break the yolks. Transfer the ramekins to the oven, and bake for 8-10 minutes or until the egg is cooked to desired taste. Remove from the oven, and cool.

Garnish with fresh parsley, and serve warm with Melba toast.

Made with chili peppers (also known as libido boosters), this recipe will bring some much-needed spice to the bedroom. Tomato, eggs, and turkey sausage with a chili-pepper kick sum up this deliciously low-calorie recipe. Serve with melba toast for a more hands-on experience.

Offer up some bedroom spooning–in a bowl, that is–when you couple fresh tomatoes and fragrant basil with quinoa and eggs for breakfast.

This savory dish makes for the ideal vegetarian, gluten-free breakfast in bed.

TOMATO-BASIL QUINOA BREAKFAST BOWL

serves 2 | prep time: 5 minutes | cook time: 25 minutes

Ingredients

2 cups water
1 cup quinoa
1 tsp. salt
1 tsp. olive oil
2 garlic cloves, diced
1 cup grape tomatoes, halved
½ cup fresh basil leaves
1 tsp. cracked black pepper
2 eggs, poached

Directions

In a medium saucepan, bring the water, quinoa, and salt to a boil. Reduce the heat to medium-low, and cover. Cook for 12-15 minutes.

Meanwhile, heat the oil in a medium skillet over medium-high. Add the garlic, and sauté until fragrant and lightly browned. Stir in the tomatoes and basil, and season with pepper. Sauté for 2-3 minutes. Remove from the heat.

Divide the quinoa between 2 small breakfast bowls. Top with the tomato-basil sauté and a poached egg.

Serve warm.

CHOCOLATE-BERRY BRUSCHETTA

serves 2 | prep time: 10 minutes | cook time: 15 minutes

Ingredients

Bruschetta
2 cups cottage cheese
½ tsp. vanilla extract
1 cup fresh strawberries, diced
½ cup blueberries
½ cup raspberries
1 ½ tsp. fresh basil, chopped
2 tbsp. chocolate vinegar

Chocolate Vinegar
5-6 semi-sweet chocolate morsels
1 cup balsamic vinegar

Directions

In a small bowl, combine the cottage cheese and vanilla. Mix well. Set aside.

In a separate bowl, toss the berries, basil, and chocolate vinegar. Serve over cottage cheese.

Chocolate Vinegar
Heat the vinegar and chocolate morsels in a small saucepan over medium-low. For approximately 5 minutes, stir until the chocolate melts. Remove from the heat, and allow to cool.

With aphrodisiac ingredients like chocolate, berries, and basil, my Chocolate-Berry Bruschetta is the ultimate breakfast-in-bed starter.

EYE CANDY

"I want to teach [people] the secret of great visual presentation. Your stomach sees the food first, and I want to help them match food flavor with the aesthetics of everything."

–Wolfgang Puck

Most chefs, myself included, believe that we all eat with our eyes. However, it turns out that we chefs are not alone. It has been said that the more appealing a food is to the eye, the more everyone tends to enjoy it. Since we eat with our eyes, I'm an avid believer that presentation is of the utmost importance when cooking for love.

So, our goal is quite simple: we should aim to seduce our mates not only with the taste of our dish, but also with its visuals. And in my opinion, no breakfast recipe is capable of doing this more than **Eggs Benedict**.

In this chapter you will find not only a quick and easy recipe for **Eggs Benedict**, but also a few of its popular variations. Adding in crab, a favorite food staple in Maryland, gives **Eggs Maryland** its regional name. Meanwhile, dishes prepared in the style of the Italian region of Florence typically feature spinach, and thus we have my **Eggs Florentine** recipe. Finally, because in Norway no meal is complete without smoked salmon, **Eggs Norwegian** consists of just that.

EGGS BENEDICT

serves 2 | prep time: 5 minutes | cook time: 10 minutes

Normally believed to have originated in Europe, the classic Eggs Benedict has roots that actually can be traced to America. Plate your Eggs Benedict with love, and be sure to drizzle your hollandaise sauce as a presentation for that perfect romantic stimulus.

Ingredients

1 tbsp. butter
8 slices Canadian bacon or deli ham
1 tsp. cracked black pepper
1 tsp. maple syrup
2 English muffins, split and toasted
4 poached eggs (p. 63)
2 tsp. chives, chopped, for garnish
butter, for English muffins

Directions

Melt the butter in a medium skillet over medium heat. Add the bacon, and sauté for 1-2 minutes, flipping occasionally. Season the bacon with black pepper, and drizzle it with syrup. Continue to sauté for 1-2 minutes or until the bacon slices are slightly browned. Remove from the heat.

Lightly butter toasted-muffin slices, and place them face up on a plate. Layer 1-2 slices of bacon on each muffin. Top the bacon with the poached eggs. Generously drizzle **Hollandaise Sauce** (p. 63) evenly over the eggs.

Garnish with chopped chives, and serve.

EGGS NORWEGIAN

serves 2 | prep time: 5 minutes | cook time: 15 minutes

Ingredients

1 tbsp. unsalted butter
1 cup fresh basil, chopped
6 eggs, beaten
4 slices smoked salmon, at room temperature
2 English muffins, split and toasted
salt and pepper, to taste

Directions

Melt the butter in a medium nonstick skillet over medium-low heat. Add the basil, and sauté until wilted. Stir in the eggs, and cook until light and fluffy. Season the eggs with salt and pepper. Remove from the heat.

Lightly butter toasted-muffin slices, and place face up on a plate. Layer a slice of salmon on each muffin. Spoon the basil scrambled eggs over the salmon. Generously drizzle *Hollandaise Sauce (p. 63)* evenly over the eggs.

Serve warm.

Take your mate on a culinary adventure to Norway when you substitute bacon with the popular Norwegian ingredient, smoked salmon. This is just as delicious when paired with basil scrambled eggs.

Serve up the romantic charm of Florence in bed with this Italian-style bread casserole with fresh spinach. Serve with hollandaise sauce for some fun, hands-on dipping.

EGGS FLORENTINE CASSEROLE

serves 4 | prep time: 1 hour, 20 minutes | cook time: 45 minutes

Ingredients

3 tbsp. extra virgin olive oil, separated
1 small onion, peeled and diced
4-5 cups chopped kale greens
8 eggs
½ cup buttermilk
1 tsp. Hungarian sweet paprika
2 tsp. ground black pepper
2 tsp. salt
1 medium loaf challah or French bread, cut into
1-inch pieces
1 cup shredded gouda cheese

Directions

Grease an 8x8 baking dish. Set aside.

Heat the oil in a medium skillet over medium. Add the onions, and sauté until fragrant and caramelized. Transfer the onions to a small bowl, and set aside.

In the same skillet, heat the remaining oil. Add the kale, and lightly season it with salt. For approximately 3-5 minutes, sauté the kale until wilted. Remove from the heat. Set aside.

In a large bowl, whisk the eggs, milk, paprika, black pepper, and 2 teaspoons of salt.

To assemble the casserole, layer the bread pieces to cover the bottom of the baking dish. Top the bread pieces with a layer of kale, cheese, onion, and additional bread. Pour the egg mixture evenly over the casserole. Cover with plastic wrap, and refrigerate for 1 hour or overnight.

Preheat the oven to 350° F.

Remove the plastic wrap from the casserole, and replace it with aluminum foil. Transfer the dish to the oven, and bake for 40-45 minutes or until set. Remove from the oven, and slice into squares.

Serve warm with *Hollandaise Sauce* (p. 63) for dipping.

EGGS MARYLAND

serves 2 | prep time: 1 hour, 45 minutes | cook time: 15 minutes

Ingredients

1 lb. lump crabmeat, crumbled
1½ tsp. salt
1½ tsp. black pepper
2 tsp. Old Bay seasoning
1 tbsp. curry powder
2 scallions, green stem only, thinly sliced
2 eggs, lightly beaten, separeated
¼ cup mayonnaise
2-3 tbsp. breadcrumbs
1 cup flour
1 cup panko breadcrumbs
1-2 cups vegetable oil, for frying
4 poached eggs (p. 63)
2 tsp. thyme
2 english muffins, split and toasted
8 asparagus stems, steamed (for garnish)

Directions

Line a baking tray with parchment paper. Set aside.

Combine the crab, salt, pepper, thyme, Old Bay seasoning, and curry powder in a medium bowl. Mix well, but avoid overmixing. Fold in the scallions, an egg, and the mayonnaise, and mix well. Add 2 tablespoons of breadcrumbs to absorb the moisture. If the crab mixture is still too wet, mix in additional tablespoons of breadcrumbs.

To form a crab cake, shape a chunk of the crab mixture into a round patty about the size of an English muffin. Transfer to the baking tray. Repeat with the remaining crab. Wrap the cakes with plastic wrap, and refrigerate for 30-60 minutes.

Pour the flour into a shallow bowl. Pour the panko breadcrumbs into a separate bowl. In a third bowl, lightly beat 1 egg. Dredge a crab cake first in the flour bowl, second in the egg bowl, and third in the panko-breadcrumb bowl. Lightly press the breadcrumbs into the cakes to ensure that they adhere. Set the cake aside on the baking tray. Repeat with the remaining cakes, and set aside.

Pour enough oil into a medium skillet to fill the skillet about halfway. Heat over medium-high to approximately 350° F. Add the cakes to the skillet, and lightly fry the cakes for about 2-3 minutes per side or until golden brown. Transfer the cakes to a paper towel-lined platter to drain any excess oil.

Lightly butter toasted-muffin slices, and place them face up on a plate. Layer a crab cake on each muffin. Top with a poached egg then generously drizzle *Hollandaise Sauce* (p. 63) evenly over the eggs. Garnish with asparagus.

Serve warm.

This mid–Atlantic take on the Eggs Benedict includes delicious crab cakes. Your mate will love the hint of curry spice in these cakes.

POACHED EGG

Ingredients

1 egg
6 cups water
1 tbsp. white vinegar

Directions

Crack the egg in a small bowl. Set aside.

Bring the water to a boil in a saucepan over high heat. Reduce the heat to medium-low, and stir in the vinegar.

Slowly pour the egg into the water, being careful not to break the yolk. Using a spoon, gently glide the egg whites toward the yolk. Allow the egg to cook for 4 minutes. Using a large, slotted spoon, gently remove the egg from the pan, allowing the water to drain.

Serve hot.

HOLLANDAISE SAUCE

4 egg yolks
1 small lemon, juiced and strained
½ cup butter, melted
1 tbsp. pepper sauce
¼ tsp. salt

In a blender, combine the egg yolks and lemon juice. Blend on high for 1-2 minutes until the mixture thickens. While blending, pour in the melted butter, pepper sauce, and salt. Continue to blend for an additional minute. Transfer the sauce to a medium glass bowl.

Add enough water to a medium saucepan to fill the pan about halfway. Bring the water to a boil over high heat.

Reduce the heat to low when the water begins to boil. Rest the glass bowl as a lid on top of the pan. Slowly stir the sauce over the simmering water for 3-4 minutes. Remove the bowl from the pan if the sauce begins to clump.

Remove from the heat, and serve warm.

SWEET HEARTS

"He who goes to bed hungry, dreams of pancakes."

-Maltese Proverb

Pancakes, French toast, waffles, and crêpes all have one sweet thing in common: all are breakfast dishes that are served with one of breakfast's most popular condiments, maple syrup. This sticky and thick liquid, consisting primarily of sugar and water, lends its sweet taste to whatever it's drizzled over. This makes maple syrup the best way to satisfy your sweetie's sweet tooth in the bedroom.

Studies show that half of all humans have an affinity for all things sugar. Whether due to hormones or genetics, science explains why we love the taste of sweet and why it can be addictive. Turns out that the taste of sugar triggers feelings of enjoyment and calms our nerves. It's also said to elicit a rush of chemicals in the body, including dopamine, which is known for its role in controlling the brain's reward and pleasure activities. Sounds to me like maple syrup, in all its sugary splendor, can help sweeten things while serving breakfast in bed.

In this chapter, I've pulled together some of my sweetest dishes to serve for breakfast. *Maple Sausage Belgian Waffles* and *Bananas Foster Maple-Cheese Crepes* are just a couple of the recipes that you can serve to your sweetheart in bed.

Why make sausage and waffles when you can make these Maple Sausage Belgian Waffles? Couple the great flavors of maple syrup and sausage with this all-in-one Belgian waffle dish. Don't forget to tempt your mate with these waffle trigangles by drizzling them with warm maple syrup.

MAPLE SAUSAGE BELGIAN WAFFLES

serves 2 | prep time: 20 minutes | cook time: 10 minutes

Ingredients

1 tbsp. butter
4 chicken-apple sausage links, casing removed
2 cups all-purpose flour, sifted
2½ tsp. baking powder
½ tsp. salt
3 tbsp. sugar
2 eggs
1¼ cups milk
2 tbsp. melted butter
butter cooking spray
maple syrup

Directions

In a small skillet, melt the butter over medium heat. Add the sausage, and sauté while crumbling the meat into small chunks. Sauté for 8-10 minutes or until the sausage is completely cooked. Transfer the sausage to a bowl. Set aside.

In a large mixing bowl, combine the flour, baking powder, salt, and sugar. Mix well.

In a small mixing bowl, whisk together the eggs, milk, and melted butter. Fold the wet ingredients into the large bowl with the dry mixture, and gently stir. Mix well.

Preheat a waffle iron, and grease it with butter cooking spray. Using a ladle, pour a spoonful of batter onto the grill of the iron. Sprinkle several sausage bits atop the waffle. Close the waffle iron, and bake until golden brown.

Serve warm with maple syrup.

BANANAS FOSTER CHEESE-STUFFED CRÊPES

serves 2 | prep time: 30 minutes | cook time: 35 minutes

Ingredients

1 cup flour
2 tbsp. sugar
¼ tsp. salt
1½ cups milk
2 eggs
1 tbsp. butter, melted
2-3 tbsp. butter, for frying, separated
powdered sugar, for dusting

Cheese Filling
1 cup ricotta cheese
¼ cup cream cheese, softened
1 tbsp. confectioners sugar
1 egg
1 tsp. lemon zest

Foster Banana Topping
½ stick unsalted butter
½ cup brown sugar
2 bananas, peeled and sliced
½ tsp. cinnamon
2 tbsp. dark rum (optional)

Directions

In a medium bowl, combine the flour, sugar, and salt. In a separate bowl, whisk together the milk, eggs, and melted butter. Combine the dry ingredients with the wet, and mix well until the batter is smooth and loose.

In a small to medium skillet, melt a tablespoon of butter over medium heat. Pour a quarter cup of batter in the center of the pan. Tilt the pan to spread the batter evenly, covering the entire surface. Allow the crêpe to cook for 2-3 minutes or until slightly browned on its bottom side. Flip the crêpe, and cook the other side until browned. Transfer the crêpe to a plate, and set aside. Repeat this step with the remaining batter for 3 additional crêpes, using an additional tablespoon of butter, if needed.

To assemble the crêpes, transfer a crêpe to a plate. Line the center of the crêpe with Cheese Filling, and fold the sides of the crepe toward the center over the filling to form an square- or rectangular-like shaped wrap (it doesn't have to be perfect). Repeat with the remaining crêpes.

Melt a tablespoon of butter in a large skillet over medium heat. Transfer the stuffed crepes to the skillet, and fry each side until golden brown (approximately 1 minute per side).

Serve the stuffed crêpes topped with hot Foster Banana and dusted with powdered sugar.

Cheese Filling
Combine all ingredients in a medium bowl. Mix well. Stuff the crêpes immediately, or store them in the refrigerator.

Foster Banana Topping
In a large skillet, melt the butter over medium

heat. Add the sugar, and stir until the sugar begins to caramelize. Add the bananas and cinnamon, and continue to stir into a thick sauce. Stir in the rum, and cook for 2 minutes. Remove from the heat and serve over crepes.

We can thank the country known for love, France, for it's thin pancakes, also known as crêpes. In this sweet and savory recipe, I've combined brown suger, banana, and ricotta cheese. Serve this sweet dish for breakfast or dessert in bed.

Philadelphia's favorite sandwich gets a French kiss for this savory breakfast makeover. French-toast hoagies stuffed with cheesy slices of steak are all but inoxicating when served with my Maple-Orange Liquer Syrup.

PHILLY CHEESE STEAK-STUFFED FRENCH TOAST

serves 2 | prep time: 15 minutes | cook time: 25 minutes

Ingredients

French Toast
2 hoagies, seeded
4 eggs
½ cup buttermilk
1 tsp. cinnamon
1 tsp. vanilla extract
2 tsp. olive oil
2 garlic cloves, minced
1 small onion, sliced
½ lb. deli roast beef, sliced into strips
1 tbsp. dried oregano
1-2 tsp. ground black pepper
salt, for taste
1 cup provolone or mozzarella cheese, shredded

Maple-Orange Liqueur Syrup
1 cup maple syrup
1 tbsp. orange zest
¼ cup orange liqueur

Directions

Using a bread knife, slice each hoagie into 1½-2" slices. Then slice the middle halfway through to create a pocket. Repeat with the remaining bread slices. Set aside.

In a large bowl, whisk the eggs, buttermilk, cinnamon, and extract. Set aside.

In a skillet, heat the oil over medium-high. Add the garlic and onions, and sauté for 2-3 minutes until the onions wilt and the garlic becomes fragrant. Add the roast beef, and season with oregano. Continue to sauté for 5 minutes or until the beef is no longer pink or red. Season the beef with black pepper, and salt to taste. Transfer the beef to a bowl to cool.

Once cooled, toss the beef strips with cheese. Stuff each bread pocket with the beef-and-cheese mixture. Place the stuffed sandwiches on a platter.

In a large skillet or stove-top griddle, melt 2 tablespoons of butter over medium heat. In batches, dip the stuffed sandwiches on each side into the egg mixture, then transfer them to the skillet. For approximately 3-4 minutes per side, cook the sandwiches until they're golden brown and the cheese melts. Remove from the griddle and serve warm with syrup.

Maple-Orange Liqueur Syrup
In a small saucepan, combine the syrup, zest, and liqueur over medium-low heat. Heat the syrup for 5-7 minutes, stirring occasionally. Remove from the heat. Serve warm.

RICOTTA PANCAKES

serves 2 | prep time: 24 hours, 10 minutes | cook time: 25 minutes

Ingredients

¾ cup fresh ricotta cheese
¼ cup milk
3 egg yolks
3 egg whites
1 tbsp. honey
1 tsp. vanilla extract
1 cup flour
1 tbsp. baking powder
1½ tbsp. sugar
¼ tsp. salt
2-3 tbsp. butter

Directions

Mix the flour, baking powder, sugar, and salt in a medium mixing bowl. In a separate larger bowl, whisk together the ricotta, milk, egg yolks, vanilla, and honey. Add the dry ingredients to the wet.

Beat the egg whites until stiff, then fold the egg whites into the batter. Avoid overbeating.

Over medium-low heat, melt the butter on a stovetop grill, flat surface facing up.

Using a ladle, spoon approximately a quarter cup of batter onto the grill. Cook the pancakes for 3-4 minutes on each side or until golden brown. Serve warm, drizzled with **Lemon-Lime Curd**.

LEMON-LIME CURD

4 egg yolks
½ cup sugar
1 tbsp. lemon zest
1 tsp. lime zest
¼ cup fresh lemon juice
¼ cup fresh lime juice
1 stick unsalted butter, cold, chopped

Combine the yolks, zests, juices, and sugar in a saucepan over medium heat. Stir continuously for 5-7 minutes until thickened.

Remove from the heat, and stir in the butter. Continue stirring until the butter melts and the mixture becomes smooth.

Transfer the curd to a small bowl, and cover with plastic wrap, making sure that the wrap is directly on top of the curd to avoid air pockets. Refrigerate until the curd thickens (1 hour to overnight).

Serve with **Ricotta Pancakes**.

Love can make us feel light and fluffy, much like these ricotta silver-dollar pancakes. Pair with maple syrup, or try them with my tangy lemon-lime curd.

BACON LOVERS

"You had me at bacon."

-Unknown

With its hypnotizing aroma, sizzling sound effects, crispy texture, and addictive salty taste, bacon easily awakens all of our senses and gets our juices flowing first thing in the morning. Surprisingly enough, however, bacon is not an aphrodisiac. Though one university study showed that students who consumed bacon experienced heightened sexual desire over non-bacon eaters, the fact still remains: no scientific proof supports the theory that bacon gets things cooking in the love department. Proof or not, bacon lovers still passionately believe in its alluring prowess.

One thing can be said about this breakfast staple, however: it's definitely a food of seduction. Canadian, maple, turkey, beef, and smoked are just a few of the types of bacon that will have most going weak in the knees from just the scent alone. Whether served as a side dish of full strips, chopped and loaded into a cheesy omelet, or wrapped around a favorite shellfish, bacon is always the main attraction at the breakfast table.

This next batch of recipes is dedicated to bacon lovers who still believe that bacon is for lovers. If you don't believe me, whip up any of these bacon recipes for your mate's breakfast in bed and conduct your own studies on their alluring affects.

BACON CHEESY PULL-APART BREAD

serves 2 | prep time: 10 minutes | cook time: 15 minutes

Ingredients

2-3 cups cheddar cheese, shredded
8-10 slices bacon, cooked and chopped
¼ cup chopped chives
1 medium round sourdough loaf

Directions

Preheat the oven to 350° F.

In a large bowl, combine the cheese, bacon, and chives. Mix well. Set aside.

Using a bread knife and without going all the way through, slice the bread in the center. Repeat with half-inch slices horizontally, then repeat vertically.

Heavily stuff the bacon, cheese, and chive mixture between cubes of sliced bread. Transfer the stuffed bread to a baking sheet, and transfer the baking sheet to the oven. For approximately 12-15 minutes, bake until the cheese melts and the bread toasts.

Remove from the oven, and serve warm.

This warm sourdough bread, loaded with cheese, bacon, and chives, makes this four-ingredient finger food a hit as a breakfast-in-bed starter. Plan on feeding one another with this delectable, hands-on dish.

Savory meets sweet when these cheddar–onion donuts are dipped in a maple glaze then topped with bacon bits. Show your love by whipping up a batch of these donuts, and serve the batch as a breakfast starter with coffee or milk.

MAPLE-BACON GLAZED DONUTS

serves 2 | prep time: 35 minutes | cook time: 20 minutes

Ingredients

3 tbsp. butter, separated
½ cup onions, chopped
1 cup white cheddar cheese, shredded
1 cup flour
1 tsp. baking powder
¼ tsp. salt
¼ cup sugar
1 egg
½ cup milk

Directions

Preheat the oven to 325° F.

In a small skillet, melt a tablespoon of butter over medium heat. Add the onions, and stir occasionally until they become translucent and begin to caramelize. Remove from heat and transfer to a small bowl. Add the cheese and mix well. Set aside.

In a medium bowl, mix the flour, baking powder, and salt. Set aside.

In a separate bowl, mix the sugar, and 2 tablespoons of butter. Add the egg and the milk, and continue to mix until combined.

Fold in the cheese-onion mixture, and mix well.

Generously grease a 6-donut pan with nonstick cooking spray. Pour the batter into the donut pan evenly between the cavities. Transfer to the oven, and bake for 12-13 minutes or until lightly browned. Remove the pan from the oven to cool.

Gently flip the pan over a large platter to remove the donuts from the pan.

MAPLE-BACON GLAZE

½ cup maple syrup
1 tsp. vanilla extract
2 tbsp. butter
1 cup confectioners sugar
½ cup bacon, cooked and crumbled

Combine the syrup, extract, and butter in a small saucepan over medium-low heat. Stir until the butter melts. Remove from the heat, and transfer the syrup to a medium bowl. Add the sugar, and whisk until smooth and creamy. Transfer the glaze to a shallow bowl for donut-glazing.

Transfer the bacon bits to a platter. Dip the top of a donut in the glaze, then dip it in the bacon bits. Gently press the donut on the bacon bits to ensure that the bacon adheres. Flip the donut, and rest it on a separate platter. Repeat with the remaining donuts, and serve.

BACON-CRUSTED MACARONI & CHEESE BALLS

serves 4 | prep time: 35 minutes | cook time: 25 minutes

Ingredients

2qts. water

1 tsp salt

16oz. box elbow macaroni

5 tbsp. unsalted butter, separated

½ cup flour

2 cups milk, warmed

1½ cups cream

1 cup smoked gouda cheese, shredded

1 cup white cheddar cheese, shredded

1 tsp. cayenne pepper

2 cups panko breadcrumbs

8 strips thick-cut bacon, cooked and chopped

2 eggs

oil for frying

Directions

Add a dash of salt to the water and bring to a boil. Add the macaroni, and cook per instructions. Drain the pasta in a colander, and transfer to a large bowl. Add a tablespoon of butter, and stir until the butter melts. Set aside.

In a large saucepan, melt 4 tablespoons of butter over medium heat. Stir in the flour and a cup of milk, whisk until smooth and free of lumps. Add the cream and remaining milk while stirring continuously. Fold in the cheeses, and continue to stir until melted. Season with the salt and cayenne pepper. Reduce the heat, and simmer for 3-5 minutes. Remove from the heat.

Fold the cheese mixture into the macaroni, and mix well. Transfer the macaroni to a baking dish and refrigerate for approximately 1 hour.

Using an ice cream scooper or spoon, scoop enough macaroni to form a small ball. Using your hand, form a ball with macaroni and cheese, and place the ball on a baking tray. Repeat with the remaining macaroni and cheese. Place macaroni-and-cheese balls in freezer until set, approximately 1 hour.

Meanwhile in a medium bowl, mix the bacon and breadcrumbs. In a separate bowl, beat the eggs.

Remove the balls from the oven. In batches, dip a ball in the eggs, then dredge the ball in the bacon-and-breadcrumbs mixture. Be sure to firmly press the breadcrumbs into the balls to ensure that they adhere. Repeat with the remaining balls.

In a large skillet, heat enough oil to fill about half of the skillet over medium-high to 350° F. Place the macaroni-and-cheese balls in the skillet, and deep fry them for 4-5 minutes or until golden brown with the center cooked through. Transfer the balls to a platter lined with paper towels to drain any excess oil, and cool. Serve warm.

These fried macaroni and cheese balls, crusted
with bacon crumbs, are ideal for brunch in
bed. Plan ahead by prepping and storing them
in your freezer to save time in the kitchen.
Remember, less time spent in the kitchen
means more time spent in the bedroom.

BACON MASCARPONE RISOTTO

serves 4 | **prep time: 20 minutes**

This bowl of warm love is a great way to get things cozy with your mate for breakfast in bed. It's creamy, cheesy, and loaded with bacon and will surely seduce the heart of any bacon lover.

Ingredients

1 cup water
1½ cups chicken stock
1 tbsp. butter
¼ tsp. cayenne pepper
dash of salt
1 tsp. ground black pepper
2 tbsp. olive oil
½ cup onions, diced
2 cups cremini mushrooms, stems removed and sliced
1 cup risotto rice
3-4 tbsp. mascarpone cheese
8 strips thick-cut bacon, cooked and chopped
2 eggs, poached

Directions

In a medium saucepan, bring a cup of water and 1½ cups of chicken stock to a boil. Add the butter, cayenne pepper, salt, and black pepper. Remove from the heat, and set aside.

Heat the oil in a large, deep skillet over medium-high. Add the onions and mushrooms, stirring occasionally until the onions become fragrant and the mushrooms tender. Add a dash of salt to the skillet, then add the rice. Continue to sauté for 3-5 minutes. Slowly stir a cup of stock into the skillet. Continue stirring while the rice cooks. When the stock reduces by half, stir in the remaining stock. Cover the skillet, and reduce the heat to medium-low. Cook the rice for 25-30 minutes or until tender.

Add the cheese and bacon to the skillet. Stir until the cheese melts and the rice mixture becomes creamy. Remove from the heat.

Serve warm with a poached or soft-boiled egg.

Watch your mate fall in love with BLTs all over again with this breakfast twist. French-toasted bread, bacon, and my spicy maple aioli are a morning pleaser.

FRENCH TOAST BLT

serves 4 | prep time: 25 minutes | cook time: 15 minutes

Ingredients

1 small loaf of sourdough or brioche bread
4 eggs
¼ cup milk
1 tbsp. orange zest
1 tsp. vanilla extract
3 tbsp. butter
1½ cups grape tomatoes, halved
1 tbsp. olive oil
1-2 tsp. cracked black pepper
2 cups lettuce, shredded
1 haas avocado, peeled and thinly sliced
10 strips thick-cut bacon, cooked medium-well
2 slices Swiss cheese (optional)

Spicy Maple Aioli
½ cup mayonnaise
2 garlic cloves, pressed
1 tbsp. maple syrup
½ tsp. cayenne pepper

Directions

Using a bread knife, slice the loaf into six ¾-inch-thick slices. Set aside.

In a large mixing bowl, whisk together the eggs, milk, zest, and extract.

Melt a tablespoon of butter over medium heat in a large skillet or griddle. In batches of 2, dip the bread slices in the egg mixture on both sides, and transfer to the skillet. Cook each side until lightly browned for approximately 2 minutes per side. Add another tablespoon of butter to the skillet,

and repeat with the remaining slices.

In a small bowl, combine the tomatoes and olive oil. Season the tomatoes with black pepper, and toss well.

To assemble the BLT, smear a dollop of Spicy Maple Aioli on a slice of toast. Top with lettuce, tomato, avocado slices, bacon strips, and cheese. Close the sandwich with a second slice of French toast.

Serve warm.

Spicy Maple Aioli
Combine all ingredients in a small bowl. Mix well. Transfer to the refrigerator to chill.

QUICKIE

"Fast sex, like fast food, is cheap, but it doesn't nourish the body–or the soul."

–Suzanne Fields

What's not to love about fast food? It's fast, and sometimes we have cravings that need that immediate gratification. After all, who wants to labor long when you can get right to the good stuff? It's also a guilty pleasure that we don't always like to admit. But most importantly, it's also very convenient. A busy schedule sometimes leaves very little room for anything else. Fast food, simply put, is a quick fix.

Yes, it seems that fast food is the quickie of the culinary arts that we can't get enough of. Fast-food lovers want to have it their way, and that normally means that it has to be finger-lickin' good. They also find themselves lovin' it at any hour and will travel just about anywhere for it, including heading for the border. Of course, if they come hungry, they will definitely want to leave happy. Ultimately, no fast-food lover wants to be left asking, "Where's the beef?"

If your mate loves fast food for breakfast, this is the perfect chapter since it's comprised of some of my favorite fast food-inspired breakfast recipes. Chicken egg biscuits, sausage burritos, and breakfast burgers are some of my favorite fast foods that you can now make right at home. Go ahead: skip the drive-thru and let these recipes satisfy your mate's guilty cravings.

Want to make your mate *happy through food*? Make it a joyful morning with this breakfast burger topped with bacon, egg, and cheese.

BREAKFAST BURGER

serves 2 | prep time: 20 minutes | cook time: 40 minutes

Ingredients

6 strips bacon
1 tsp. olive oil
1 small onion, sliced
½ lb. ground meat (beef, turkey, or pork)
1 tbsp. black pepper
2 tsp. salt
1 packet onion soup mix
1 egg
3-4 tbsp. ketchup
½ cup breadcrumbs
4 slices Swiss cheese (or your favorite)
2 bagels, sliced and toasted
2 tbsp. mayonnaise
lettuce and tomato, as condiments
2 eggs, fried

Directions

Preheat the oven to 350° F.

Line the bacon strips on a baking tray. Transfer to the oven, and bake until cooked. Remove from the oven, and transfer the bacon to a platter lined with a paper towel. Set aside.

In a small skillet, heat the oil over medium. Add the onions, and sauté until translucent and caramelized. Remove from the heat, and transfer to a small bowl. Set aside.

In a medium bowl, season the ground meat with the salt and black pepper. Add the onion soup mix, egg, ketchup, and breadcrumbs. Lightly knead the ingredients into the meat. If the meat is very moist, add an additional tablespoon of breadcrumbs.

Shape the ground meat into 2 burger patties. Grease a stovetop grill, and heat over medium-high. Transfer the burgers to the grill, and cook to desired wellness. While on the grill, top each burger with cheese to melt.

To assemble the breakfast burger, lightly spread 1 side of each bagel with mayonnaise. Place the lettuce and tomato slices on 1 bagel half, then the cheeseburger, bacon, grilled onions, and fried egg on the other.

Close the burger, and serve warm.

CHICKEN & EGG BISCUITS

serves 2-3 | prep time: 40 minutes | cook time: 30 minutes

Ingredients

2 boneless chicken breasts, thinly sliced
1 tsp. salt
1 cup flour
1 tsp. onion powder
1 tsp. garlic powder
½ tsp. cayenne pepper
2 eggs
2 cups breadcrumbs
¼ cup parmesan cheese
2 tbsp. dried oregano
½ tsp. ground black pepper
4 eggs, scrambled
vegetable oil, for frying

Sweet Butter Biscuits
1 tbsp. brown sugar
½ cup butter, melted
2 cups flour, sifted
2 tsp. baking powder
1 tbsp. granulated sugar
½ tsp. salt
4 tbsp. shortening, crumbled
¾ cup milk

Directions

Slice the chicken breasts in half to create 4 even slices. Season the chicken with the salt and ground black pepper.

To bread the chicken, prepare a breading station by aligning 3 medium bowls in a row. Combine the flour, garlic, onion powder, and cayenne pepper in 1 bowl. Mix well. In another bowl, whisk the eggs. In a third bowl, combine the breadcrumbs, Parmesan cheese, and oregano. Mix well.

One at a time, dip the chicken pieces into the seasoned flour. Coat well. Then dip the chicken into the eggs, making sure to cover the entire chicken. Next, dredge the chicken in the breadcrumbs, slightly pressing so that the crumbs adhere to chicken. Transfer to a platter, and repeat with the remaining chicken.

In a large skillet filled to about half-full, heat vegetable oil over moderately high. Transfer the chicken to the skillet, and fry for approximately 2-3 minutes on each side, turning once, until cooked through and golden brown.

Transfer the chicken to a platter lined with a paper towel to drain any excess oil. Serve warm with Sweet Butter Biscuits and scrambled eggs.

Sweet Butter Biscuits
Preheat the oven to 400° F. Grease a baking sheet, and set aside.

Combine the brown sugar and butter in a small bowl. Mix well, and set aside. Combine the flour, baking powder, granulated sugar, and salt in a mixing bowl. Add the shortening. Add the milk gradually, stirring until a soft dough is formed.

Transfer the dough to a slightly floured board, and lightly knead for 30 seconds. Roll the dough out to about a half-inch thick, and cut with a floured biscuit cutter. Transfer the biscuits to the baking sheet, and bake for 12 minutes or until lightly browned. Remove the biscuits from the oven, and

lightly brush with the sugar-butter mixture. Return the biscuits to the oven, and bake for additional 2-3 minutes or until golden brown. Remove from the oven to cool.

Serve warm.

Your mate will quickly want to *eat more chicken* when you whip up these Chicken & Egg Biscuits for breakfast in bed.

You and your mate get to *have it your way* when you serve up a batch of these French toast nuggets for breakfast.

GRANOLA FRENCH TOAST NUGGETS

serves 2 | prep time: 20 minutes | cook time: 20 minutes

Ingredients

4 eggs
½ cup milk
1 tsp. vanilla extract
1 tsp. cinnamon
2 tbsp. orange zest
1½ cups granola
1 small challah bread loaf, cut into 1" cubes
3-4 tbsp. butter
powdered sugar, for dusting
maple syrup

Directions

Whisk the eggs in a large mixing bowl. Stir in the milk, extract, cinnamon, and zest. Transfer the granola to a medium platter. Working in batches, dip the bread cubes into the egg mixture, coating all sides. Dredge the cubes in the granola, pressing the granola into the bread to ensure that it adheres. Transfer the cubes to a platter lined with wax paper.

Over medium heat, melt a tablespoon of butter in a large skillet or griddle. In batches, transfer the cubes to the skillet, and fry each piece until golden brown, flipping occasionally. Repeat with the remaining bread cubes.

Dust the cubes with powdered sugar, and serve with maple syrup.

SPICY CHORIZO BREAKFAST BURRITOS

serves 2 | prep time: 40 minutes | cook time: 25 minutes

Ingredients

4 spicy chorizo sausage links, chopped
6 eggs, beaten
2 large flour tortillas
½ cup pinto beans, drained and rinsed
½ white cheddar cheese, shredded
¼ cup monterey pepper jack cheese, shredded
¼ cup pico de gallo (recipe below)
2 tbsp. unsalted butter, separated
1 tsp. salt
1 tsp. ground black pepper
avocado, as condiment
lime wedges, as condiment

Pico de Gallo

¼ cup finely chopped red bell pepper
¼ cup finely chopped yellow bell pepper
2 jalapeño peppers, diced
1 small onion, peeled and diced
1 medium tomato, diced
2-3 tbsp. finely chopped fresh cilantro

Directions

Combine all ingredients for the pico de gallo in a medium bowl, and toss well. Keep refrigerated.

Preheat the oven to 400° F. Grease a baking sheet, and set aside.

Melt a tablespoon of butter over medium heat in a medium skillet. Add the sausage to the skillet, and sauté while breaking the sausage into crumbles for 4-5 minutes or until cooked through. Remove the skillet from the heat, and set aside.

Melt another tablespoon of butter over medium heat in the medium skillet. Add the pico de gallo and beans. Season the ingredients with the salt and pepper, and sauté until the onions become translucent. Reduce the heat to low, and add the eggs, cheese, and sausage. Continuously stir the eggs, and cook until fluffy.

Meanwhile, to toast the tortillas, grease a separate pan with cooking spray, and warm over medium heat. Add a tortilla to the skillet, and toast each side for approximately 1 minute. Repeat with the second tortilla.

To wrap the burritos, transfer a tortilla to a platter. Line the center of the tortilla with the chorizo-egg scramble, and wrap the burrito. Serve warm with lime wedges and/or avocado slices.

Is your mate *deserving of a love break today?* Wrap your mate up in love with this spicy sausage burrito.

SOUTHERN COMFORTS

"Food, like a loving touch or a glimpse of divine power, has the ability to comfort."

-Norman Kolpas

Contrary to popular belief, comfort food isn't necessarily synonymous with food of the South. In fact, a recent study found that comfort food is less about the region and more about relationships and positive memories of family and social events. It seems that comfort food is not only shared in the name of love, but also made with love; and of course, Southern cuisine, especially, qualifies as food made with love. From the seasoning and battering of fried chicken to the slow-stirred pot of grits, Southern cooking requires that special, hands-on approach when expressing your love through food.

How exactly is comfort food ideal for breakfast in bed? Well, for one, comfort food can be quite hearty, which almost guarantees that your mate will stay in the sack. Whether served savory or sweet, it elicits feelings of wanting to curl up while being held, paving the way for some much-desired cuddling and spooning. But my personal favorite feature of comfort food has to be its ability to remind us of a sentimental value, and when served for breakfast in bed, it almost guarantees an unforgettable morning with your mate.

For this hearty chapter, you will find my take on Southern-inspired breakfast recipes from **Fried Jerk Chicken & Waffles** to **Jerk Shrimp & Grits**. If you're looking for recipes for snuggling, these are it.

JERK SHRIMP & GRITS

serves 2 | prep time: 30 minutes | cook time: 45 minutes

Ingredients

Jerk Shrimp
12 large shrimp, peeled and de-veined
1 tbsp. fresh ginger
1 tbsp. allspice
1 tsp. cinnamon
¼ tsp. ground black pepper
1 tbsp. old bay seasoning
1 tsp. vinegar
2 tsp. low sodium soy sauce
2 tbsp. jerk seasoning, separated
6 thick-cut bacon strips, cut in half
2 tbsp. olive oil
2 garlic cloves, minced
1 small onion, peeled and diced
½ cup green pepper, diced
½ cup yellow pepper, diced
½ cup red pepper, diced
1 cup chicken stock

Creamy Grits
1 cup water
1 cup half-and-half
1 tbsp. unsalted butter
½ cup grits
salt, to taste

Directions

Preheat the oven to 350° F. Lightly grease a baking sheet. Set aside.
In a medium bowl, season the shrimp with the ginger, allspice, cinnamon, black pepper, and Old Bay seasoning. Add the vinegar, soy sauce, and a tablespoon of jerk seasoning. Rub onto the shrimp.

Line a half strip of bacon on a flat surface. Place a shrimp at one end of the bacon, and wrap the shrimp with the bacon, rolling the shrimp from one end of the bacon to the other. Transfer the bacon-wrapped shrimp to the baking sheet. Repeat.

Transfer the baking sheet to the oven, and bake for 20-25 minutes or until the bacon is golden brown.

Meanwhile, heat the olive oil over medium-high in a large skillet. Add the garlic and onion, and sauté for approximately 2-3 minutes. Add the peppers, and stir for 2 minutes. Stir in a tablespoon of jerk seasoning and the chicken stock. Reduce the heat to medium-low. Cover and simmer for 5-7 minutes until the sauce thickens. Transfer the shrimp to the skillet, and toss the shrimp in the sauce. Cover and simmer for 5 minutes.

Creamy Grits
Bring the water and half-and-half to a boil in a medium saucepan over medium-high heat. Reduce the heat to medium, and stir in the butter and grits. Continue stirring until the grits thicken. Season the grits with salt to taste.

Remove from the heat, and serve.

Introduce some Jamaican spice to the bedroom with this Caribbean twist on the Southern breakfast classic. Serve my shrimp, wrapped in bacon and smothered in jerk gravy, over grits for the ultimate comforting breakfast.

Satisfy that morning sweet tooth with this dessert–like breakfast starter. A natural aphrodisiac for men, the peach is a sexy fruit known for conjuring up ideas of making whoopee.

CINNAMON BISCUIT PEACH COBBLER

serves 2 | prep time: 30 minutes | cook time: 25 minutes

Ingredients

Biscuit Dough
2 cups flour
2 tbsp. baking powder
2 tbsp. granulated white sugar
½ tsp. salt
6 tbsp. butter, cubed
¾ cup milk
1 tbsp butter, melted
1 tsp. ground cinnamon

Peach Filling
1 tbsp. butter
½ cup brown sugar
2 tsp. lemon zest
¼ tsp. ground nutmeg
2 tbsp. flour
1 cup water
1 tsp. vanilla extract
1 can peaches in heavy syrup

Directions

Preheat the oven to 350° F. Keep the ingredients for the biscuit dough and for the peach filling separate.

In a large mixing bowl, combine the flour, baking powder, sugar, salt, and cubed butter from the biscuit ingredients. Mix well. Gradually add the milk, stirring until the dough is formed.

Roll the dough out onto a slightly floured board, and lightly knead for 30 seconds. Transfer to a bowl, and cover with a cloth. Let the dough sit for approximately 25 minutes to rise.

Meanwhile, in a medium saucepan, melt the butter from the peach filling ingredients over medium heat. Add the sugar, zest, and nutmeg. Stir until the sugar begins to caramelize. Add the flour, water, and extract to the saucepan. Increase the heat to medium-high, and continue stirring until the mixture thickens. Add the peaches in heavy syrup. Reduce the heat to low, and simmer for 2-3 minutes. Remove from the heat, and set aside.

Once the dough has risen, return the dough to the board, and roll or pat the dough into a half-inch-thick square or circle. Using a biscuit cutter or ramekin, cut 4 biscuits from the dough, and set aside.

In a small bowl, combine the melted butter and cinnamon. Mix well, and set aside.

Filling each about halfway, spoon the peach filling evenly into 4 ramekins. Top each ramekin with a biscuit. Brush each biscuit top with the cinnamon-butter. Transfer to the oven, and bake for 25 minutes or until the biscuit becomes golden brown.

Remove from the oven, and brush the biscuit tops with the cinnamon-butter once again. Serve warm.

FRIED JERK CHICKEN & WAFFLES

serves 2 | prep time: 25 minutes | cook time: 10 minutes

Ingredients

2 tbsp. ground allspice
2 tbsp. ginger powder
1 tbsp. cinnamon
1 tbsp. brown sugar
1 tbsp. cumin
1 tbsp. garlic powder
1 tbsp. onion powder
2 tbsp. red pepper flakes
3 boneless chicken breasts, cut into 1" tenders
2 tbsp. ground black pepper
1-2 tbsp. salt
2 cups flour
2 large eggs
2-3 cups panko breadcrumbs
vegetable oil for frying

Directions

In small bowl, combine the allspice, ginger powder, cinnamon, sugar, cumin, garlic, onion powder, and pepper flakes to create a jerk rub. Mix well.

Transfer the chicken tenders to a medium bowl, and season with the salt and pepper. Season the tenders with the jerk rub, and set aside.

Transfer the flour to a medium bowl or platter. In batches, dredge the tenders in the flour. Set aside.

Whisk the eggs in a medium bowl. In a separate medium bowl, add the breadcrumbs.

One at a time, dip a tender into the egg mixture, then transfer it to the bowl of breadcrumbs. Dredge the tender while slightly pressing to ensure that the crumbs adhere. Repeat with the remaining tenders, and set aside.

In a large skillet or deep fryer, heat the oil to 350° F. Transfer the tenders to the skillet, and fry over moderately high heat until cooked through and golden brown, turning once for about 3 minutes per side.

Transfer the tenders to a paper towel to drain any excess oil. Serve warm with **Belgian Waffles with Apple Compote** (p. 105).

Spice meets sweet when my signature jerk fried chicken is paired with Belgian Waffles topped with a healthy serving of warm Apple Compote.

BELGIAN WAFFLES WITH APPLE COMPOTE

serves 2 | prep time: 25 minutes | cook time: 20 minutes

Ingredients

Belgian Waffles
2 cups all-purpose flour
½ cup sugar
4 tsp. baking powder
1 tsp. salt
2 egg yolks
2 egg whites
2 cups milk
½ cup vegetable oil
1 tbsp. orange zest
cooking spray

Apple Compote
2 apples, peeled and sliced into wedges
2 tbsp. sugar
1 tsp. cinnamon
1 tsp. nutmeg
2 tbsp. butter

Directions

Combine the flour, sugar, baking powder, and salt in a large mixing bowl. In a separate bowl, whisk the egg yolks, milk, and oil. Add the liquid mixture to the dry. Mix well. Stir in the orange zest.

In a small bowl, beat the egg whites until frothy and stiff. Fold the egg whites into the batter.

Grease the grill of a waffle iron with butter cooking spray. Using a ladle, pour a spoonful of batter onto the grill. Cook until the waffle is golden brown. Repeat with the remaining batter.

In a medium bowl, season the wedges with sugar, cinnamon, and nutmeg. In a medium saucepan, melt the butter over medium heat. Add the apple wedges to the pan, and sauté for 8-10 minutes or until the sugar browns.

Serve the waffles and compote warm with **Fried Jerk Chicken** (p. 102).

105

Quick, simple, and delicious best describe these fish cakes. Serve with eggs, grits, and love for the full Southern-breakfast experience.

SALMON CROQUETTES

serves 4 | prep time: 10 minutes | cook time: 10 minutes

Ingredients

12oz. can Alaskan pink salmon, drained and
flaked with skin and bones removed
2 tsp. salt
1 tbsp. ground black pepper
1 tbsp. Old Bay seasoning
3 garlic cloves, minced or pressed
¼ cup onion, diced
1 tbsp. fresh thyme
1 egg, lightly beaten
2-4 tbsp. breadcrumps
vegetable oil for frying

Directions

In a mixing bowl, season the salmon with the salt, pepper, and Old Bay seasoning. Add the garlic, onion, and thyme. Mix well. Fold in the egg, and mix well. Add 2 tablespoons of breadcrumbs to absorb some of the moisture. Mix well. Add more breadcrumbs to further reduce the moisture, if necessary.

Shape the salmon into 4 medium-sized balls, then slightly flatten them into cakes. Transfer to a plate, and cover with plastic wrap. Refrigerate for 30 minutes.

In a large skillet, enough to fill it halfway, heat the oil over high. Lightly fry the cakes on each side for approximately 3-4 minutes, flipping only once. Remove the cakes from the skillet, and transfer to a plate covered with paper towels.

Serve warm.

BISCUITS & SAUSAGE GRAVY

serves 4 | prep time: 15 minutes | cook time: 40 minutes

Ingredients

1 tsp. olive oil
4 turkey sausage links, casings removed
1 tsp. ground black pepper
1 tbsp. fresh sage, minced
2 garlic cloves, minced
1½ cups half-and-half
4 tbsp. butter
½ cup diced shallots or onions
4 tbsp. all-purpose flour
½ tsp. cayenne pepper
salt, to taste

Directions

In a small skillet, heat the oil over medium. Add the sausage, and stir until cooked through. Season the sausage with the black pepper, stir in the sage and garlic. Continue to stir until the garlic becomes fragrant. Remove from the heat, and set aside.

In a small saucepan, warm the half-and-half over medium-low heat. Reduce the heat to keep warm.

In a medium saucepan, melt the butter over medium heat. Add the diced shallots, and sauté for 3 minutes. Add the flour, and stir for 1 minute. Add the warm half-and-half, and continue to stir for approximately 7-10 minutes until the mixture thickens into a gravy. Stir in the sausage, cayenne pepper, and salt to taste. Reduce the heat to low. Cover and simmer for 5 minutes.

Serve warm with **Cheese Biscuits**.

CHEESE BISCUITS

2 cups flour, sifted
2 tsp. baking powder
½ tsp. salt
1 tbsp. sugar
4 tbsp. shortening, chopped
½ cup gruyere cheese, shredded
¾ cup milk

In a mixing bowl, combine the flour, baking powder, salt, and sugar. Add the shortening, then cheese. Gradually add the milk, stirring until a soft dough is formed. Roll out the dough onto a floured board, and lightly knead for 30 seconds. Don't over-knead. With a rolling pin, roll the dough to about a half-inch thick. Using a 2-inch floured biscuit-cutter, cut approximately 6-8 biscuits from the dough.

Transfer to a baking sheet. Align the biscuits so that they touch. Transfer to the oven, and bake for 12 minutes. Remove from the oven, and lightly brush the biscuits with melted butter. Return the biscuits to the oven, and bake for an additional 3 minutes. Remove the sheet from the oven to cool. Using a fork, cut each biscuit open, and transfer to a serving platter. Top biscuits with sausage gravy.

Serve warm.

Some cuddling and cozy times will lie ahead after serving up this "stick to your ribs" Southern–breakfast staple.

TEASE THE SEASON

"What nicer thing can you do for somebody than make them breakfast."

-Anthony Bourdain

I have to agree with Anthony Bourdain. Making breakfast is probably one of the most scrumptious things you can do for a loved one. I liken it to the act of gift-giving. However, instead of a pretty box wrapped with a ribbon, the recipient gets a heavenly experience that will last a lifetime. After all, gift-giving is an expression of love, so what better way to express this love than with a palatable treat? While recipients of this yummy surprise will feel good in their tummies, givers of the delicious gift will feel a sense of euphoria too. Elation, coincidentally enough, is very similar to the feeling we experience when making whoopee.

How is this possible? Well, science links the act of giving to the release of a hormone within our bodies called oxytocin. This hormone, which is released during nooky, stirs up that warm feeling and connection to others within us. Sounds like whetting your mate's appetite with breakfast in bed can really get you both in the mood.

The next batch of recipes is designed in the spirit of gift-giving. For Valentine's Day, show your love with sweet **Strawberry-Lemon Scones** or a tempting **French Toast Bake** drizzled with **Red Velvet Syrup**. In autumn, delight your mate with aromatic **Pumpkin Oat Pancakes** or **Apple-Pumpkin Muffins**. Also, try repurposing some of that holiday stuffing with my savory **Bacon-Wrapped Stuffin' Muffins**!

Gift-giving is contagious. Give the gift of breakfast, and chances are you'll receive a post-breakfast gift from your mate in return.

CREAM CHEESE FRENCH TOAST BAKE

serves 4 | prep time: 1.5 hours | cook time: 1 hour

Ingredients

French Toast

1 French bread, sliced into 1" slices
½ cup cream cheese, softened
6 eggs
1½ cups half-and-half
2 tbsp. orange zest
¼ cup maple syrup
1 tsp. vanilla extract
2 tsp. ground cinnamon
confectioners sugar for garnish

Red Velvet Syrup

1 cup water
1 cup sugar
½ cup cocoa beans
1 tbsp. red food coloring

Directions

Grease an 8x8 baking dish and set aside.

Spread each slice of bread with a thin layer of cream cheese, then slice the bread into cubes. Transfer the cubes to the baking dish. Set aside.

To make the custard, whisk together the eggs, half-and-half, zest, syrup, extract, and cinnamon in a medium bowl. Evenly pour the egg mixture over the bread cubes. With a spoon, press into the bread cubes to absorb all of the custard. Cover with plastic wrap, and refrigerate for 1-24 hours.

Preheat the oven to 350° F.

Remove the plastic wrap from the casserole, and re-cover with aluminum foil. Transfer to the oven, and bake for 30-35 minutes. Remove the foil covering, and bake for an additional 15 minutes or until lightly browned. Remove from the oven, and slice into squares.

Red Velvet Syrup

In a small saucepan, bring the water, sugar, and beans to a boil. Reduce the heat to medium-low, and stir. After the sugar has fully dissolved, remove the pan from the heat. Strain the beans from the liquid in a small bowl. Discard beans and return liquid to saucepan. Add the food coloring and stir until the syrup is fully red and thickens (approx. 5-7 minutes).

Serve warm.

Show your mate some red–hot love when you drizzle my homemade Red Velvet Syrup all over this easy, make–ahead French Toast bake.

Whisk your love across the pond for Valentine's Day with these sweet British teacakes stuffed with fresh strawberry–lemon filling.

STRAWBERRY–LEMON SCONES

serves 2 | prep time: 35 minutes | cook time: 15 minutes

Ingredients

cooking spray
1½ cups flour
⅓ cup sugar
1 tbsp. baking powder
¼ tsp. salt
1 tbsp. thyme
4 tbsp. butter, chilled and cut into small cubes
⅓ cup milk
5-6 strawberries, diced and de-stemmed
1 tsp. lemon zest
2 tbsp. strawberry jam

Directions

Preheat the oven to 350° F.

Grease a baking sheet with butter cooking spray. Set aside.

In a medium bowl, combine the flour, sugar, baking powder, salt, and thyme. Mix well. Add the butter cubes. Using your hands, grind the butter in the flour mixture until the butter resembles small grains. While stirring the flour mixture, add the milk to form dough. Cover the dough, and let it sit for 20 minutes to rise.

Meanwhile, to make the strawberry-lemon filling, transfer the strawberries to a small bowl. Add the zest and jam. Mix well, and set aside.

Roll the dough out onto a floured surface, and roll into a ball. Divide the ball into 4 smaller balls. Create a deep dimple in the middle of 1 of the balls. Fill the dimple with a teaspoon of strawberry filling. Fold the ball closed, and transfer it to the baking sheet. Repeat with the remaining balls.

Bake for 12-15 minutes or until the scones are slightly browned. Remove from the oven to cool.

Serve warm or at room temperature.

This fresh-baked breakfast starter, combining apple and pumpkin spice, gets more than just breakfast started when served in bed.

SPICED APPLE–PUMPKIN MUFFINS

serves 6 | prep time: 20 minutes | cook time: 15 minutes

Ingredients

butter cooking spray
2 cups flour
1½ tsp. baking powder
1½ tsp. baking soda
1 tsp. salt
1 tsp. ginger
1 tsp. clove
½ tsp. nutmeg
½ tsp. cinnamon
2 eggs
1 cup milk
½ cup butter, melted
1 cup brown sugar
¾ cup pumpkin puree
¼ cup applesauce

Directions

Preheat the oven to 375° F. Grease a 24-cup muffin pan with cooking spray. Set aside.

In a medium bowl, combine the flour, baking powder, baking soda, salt, ginger, clove, nutmeg, and cinnamon. Mix well, and set aside.

In a large bowl, whisk together the eggs, milk, butter, sugar, puree, and applesauce. Gradually stir in the flour mixture a quarter cup at a time. Stir the batter until well-combined.

Using a tablespoon, spoon the batter evenly into muffin cups to about three-quarters full. Be careful not to overfill the cups.

Transfer to the oven, and bake for 12-15 minutes or until golden brown. Remove from the oven to cool.

Remove the muffins from the pan, and serve warm.

SPICED PUMPKIN OAT PANCAKES

serves 2 | prep time: 20 minutes | cook time: 10 minutes

Ingredients

1 cup flour
¾ cup quick oats
3 tbsp. sugar
1 tbsp. baking powder
½ tsp. salt
½ tsp. ginger
1 tsp allspice
½ tsp. nutmeg
½ tsp. cinnamon
1¼ cup almond milk
1 egg
½ cup pumpkin purée
¼ tsp. vanilla extract
2 tbsp. melted butter
1 tbsp. butter
2 tbsp. fresh whipped cream
¼ cup pecans, crushed for garnish (optional)
maple syrup

Directions

In a large bowl, combine the flour, oats, sugar, baking powder, salt, ginger, allspice, nutmeg, and cinnamon. Mix well, and set aside.

In separate medium bowl, combine the milk, egg, pumpkin puree, extract, and melted butter. Mix well.

Transfer the liquid mixture to the dry mixture, and stir into batter. Transfer the batter to a large measuring cup for easy pouring.

Melt the butter over medium-low heat on a stovetop grill with the flat surface facing up. Be sure to grease the entire surface of the pan. Pour a small amount of batter (approximately a quarter cup) onto the grill to form a medium-sized pancake. Repeat with the remaining batter. Cook the pancakes for 2-3 minutes on each side or until golden brown. Flip the pancakes only once; do not flatten them with a spatula.

Serve the pancakes warm with syrup and a dollop of whipped cream. Garnish with the pecans.

The spice is right! Give your love a special gift this pumpkin season with these Spiced Pumpkin Oat Pancakes.

Repurpose some of that holiday love for a breakfast-in-bad treat with these post-holiday Stuffin' Muffins. Made with leftover stuffing, these muffins are wrapped in bacon for a delicious, day-after twist.

BACON-WRAPPED STUFFIN' MUFFINS

serves 3 | prep time: 15 minutes | cook time: 25 minutes

Ingredients

3 cups cooked stuffing
2 tbsp. fresh basil, chopped
2 tbsp. havarti cheese, chopped
cooking spray
6 slices thick-cut bacon

Directions

Preheat the oven to 350° F.

In a medium bowl, combine the stuffing, basil, and cheese. Toss well. Set aside.

Lightly grease the bottom of a 6-cup muffin pan with cooking spray. Line the inside of a muffin cup with a bacon strip. Firmly press the bacon to the sides of the cup. Spoon about a half-cup of stuffing to the muffin cups. Repeat with the remaining cups.

Transfer to the oven, and bake for 20-25 minutes or until the bacon is cooked medium to well. Remove from the oven. Use a fork or knife to gently loosen the muffins.

Remove muffins from the pan, and serve warm.

MEAT LOVERS STROMBOLI

serves 2 | prep time: 15 minutes | cook time: 25 minutes

Ingredients

1½ cups fresh mozzarella, shredded
1 tbsp. basil, diced
1 tsp. cracked black pepper
2 tsp. olive oil, separated
3 links breakfast sausage
15oz. fresh pizza dough
4-5 strips bacon, cooked and chopped
3-4 slices deli ham, diced
1 tbsp. butter, melted
½ cup crushed tomato
2 tbsp. fresh basil, chopped

Directions

Preheat the oven to 350° F. Lightly grease a baking sheet with cooking spray. Set aside.

In a small bowl, combine the cheese, a teaspoon of oil, the basil, and the black pepper. Toss well. Set aside.

Dice the sausage links into half-inch chunks. Heat the oil in a small skillet over medium. Add the breakfast sausage, and sauté until cooked. Remove from the heat, and set aside.

On a lightly floured surface, roll the dough out into a circle. Line the center of the dough with the cheese-basil mixture, ham, bacon, and sausage. Roll the dough to form a Stromboli, making sure to seal it closed. Using a knife, cut 3-4 slits across the top.

Transfer to the baking sheet, and brush the top of the Stromboli with butter. Transfer the sheet to the oven, and bake for 12-15 minutes or until the dough is fully cooked and lightly browned.

Remove from the oven, and slice. Serve warm with the crushed tomato and basil.

Breakfast meats–including bacon, sausage, and ham–are the hidden gifts found inside this quick and easy stromboli. Remember, less time in the kitchen means more time for your mate to thank you for those expected and unexpected gifts.

COQUITO

serves 4 | prep time: 2 hours, 5 minutes

If you're looking to spread some Christmas cheer, it will definitely be a Feliz Navidad when you serve this Puerto Rican-inspired coconut eggnog. This festive drink is equally delicious whether you serve it spiked or virgin. When paired with my *Baked Eggnog Donuts*, seconds are always guaranteed.

Ingredients

1-2 cups white rum
14oz. can condensed milk
12oz. can evaporated milk
15oz. can cream of coconut
1 tsp. vanilla extract
½ tsp. cinnamon
whipped cream, for garnish
cinnamon stick, for garnish

Directions

Mix all ingredients in a blender for approximately 45 seconds. Refrigerate for a minimum of 2 hours.

Shake, and serve chilled. Top with whipped cream and a Cinnamon Stick if desired.

RUM-GLAZED EGGNOG DONUTS

serves 3 | prep time: 15 minutes | cook time: 15 minutes

Ingredients

Eggnog Donuts
1 cup flour
1 tsp. baking powder
½ tsp. grated nutmeg
¼ tsp. clove
¼ tsp. salt
¼ cup sugar
2 tbsp. butter
1 egg
½ cup eggnog

Eggnog Rum Glaze
2 tbsp. eggnog
1 tbsp. rum
½ cup powdered sugar

Directions

Preheat the oven to 325° F.

In a medium bowl, combine the flour, baking powder, nutmeg, clove, and salt. Mix well, and set aside. In a separate bowl, combine the sugar and butter. Mix well. Stir in the egg and eggnog. Add the flour mixture, and mix until combined.

Generously grease a 6-hole donut pan with nonstick cooking spray. Transfer the batter evenly among the 6 cups of the pan. Transfer the pan to the oven, and bake for 12-13 minutes.

Meanwhile, to prepare the glaze, stir the powdered sugar, rum, and eggnog until combined.

Remove the donuts from the oven, and immediately brush the glaze directly onto them. Dust with additional nutmeg.

Serve warm.

BREAKFAST AFTER DARK

"Garnish your food with romance."

–Amanda Mosher

By now, we all know that there's an obvious and strong connection between romance and food. With the growing popularity of breakfast, more and more lovers are finding themselves planning the perfect romantic breakfast for dinner. However, this begs the question: what does one serve for a deliciously romantic breakfast? Easy! It should include the same sensual dishes that we typically associate with a romantic dinner—teasing all of our senses while evoking feelings of love and intimacy.

Similar to lovemaking, eating requires that we use all of our senses, so try to choose sexy dishes that ignite your mate's sight, touch, sound, smell, and without question, taste. From the sunny-side up egg with its tender whites surrounding that golden yoke, to hot finger foods with a creamy dipping sauce—along with my personal favorite, the sizzling dish of a hot and steamy skillet—believe me, you can never go wrong with tickling the five senses.

Different regions of the world inspire the following breakfast-for-dinner recipes. The **Greek Omelet**, my **Thai Spicy Basil Breakfast Fried Rice**, the **Shrimp and Rice Pottage**, and my **Curry Salmon & Coconut Grits** are just a few dinner-turned-breakfast meals that will send you and your mate on a steamy, culinary adventure.

CURRY SALMON

serves 2 | prep time: 25 minutes | cook time: 45 minutes

Ingredients

1 lb. salmon fillet, skinned and cubed
1 tsp. salt
2 tsp. black pepper
1 tbsp. Old Bay seasoning
2 tsp. cumin powder
2 tbsp. curry powder
2 tbsp. vegetable oil
1 large onion, sliced
3 garlic cloves, minced
2 tbsp. corn meal or flour
3 bay leaves
1 Scotch bonnet pepper (optional)
1 cup coconut milk
½ cup water

Directions

In a bowl, season the salmon with the salt, black pepper, Old Bay seasoning, cumin, and curry powder. Set aside.

In a large pan, heat the oil on medium-high. Add the onions and garlic. Sauté until the onions become translucent. Stir in the flour, bay leaves, scotch bonnet pepper, coconut milk, and water. Mix well. Reduce the heat to medium, and cover to simmer for 15 minutes or until the gravy thickens.

Stir in the salmon. Reduce the heat to low, and cover to simmer for an additional 15 minutes or until the salmon is cooked through.

Remove the bay leaves and scotch bonnet pepper, and discard.

Serve the salmon warm over **Coconut Grits**.

COCONUT GRITS

1 cups water
1 cup coconut milk
2 tbsp. butter
1 cup stone ground white grits
¼ tsp. salt
¼ tsp. black pepper

Bring the water and milk to a boil in a medium saucepan. Add the butter, salt, and pepper to the pan. Stir in the grits. Reduce the heat to medium-low, and stir until the grits begin to thicken. Remove from the heat.

Serve warm.

While this "curry in a hurry" breakfast dish may be quick to prepare, its romantic hold on your mate will be long-lasting.

Aphrodite, the goddess of love, would definitely approve of these Greek-inspired, breakfast-for-dinner recipes. Both are wrapped in love and phyllo dough.

WRAPPED GREEK OMELET

serves 2 | prep time: 20 minutes | cook time: 25 minutes

Ingredients

6 eggs
¼ cup milk
¼ tsp. salt
½ tsp. black pepper
1 tbsp. fresh dill, diced
2 tbsp. butter
1 small onion, peeled and diced
2 cups fresh spinach, chopped
1 medium tomato, seeded and chopped
6 phyllo pastry sheets, 14x18"
¼ cup melted butter
¾ cup feta cheese, crumbled

Directions

Preheat the oven to 350° F. Line a baking tray with wax paper, and set aside.

In a large bowl, whisk together the eggs, milk, salt, pepper, and dill. Set aside.

Melt the butter in a large nonstick skillet over medium heat. Add the onions, and sauté for 2-3 minutes. Add the spinach, and stir for approximately 3 minutes until the spinach reduces. Stir in the egg mixture. Using a spoon, stir the eggs until scrambled and fluffy. Stir in the tomatoes, and continue to cook for 2 minutes.

Remove from the heat, and set aside.

Gently place a pastry sheet on a flat surface, and brush the sheet with melted butter. Place another sheet on top of the first, and brush it with butter. Repeat with the remaining sheets.

Spoon the scrambled eggs along the center of the pastry sheets. Sprinkle the eggs with feta cheese. Fold the pastry horizontally, and roll the eggs into a cylindrical wrap. With each fold, lightly brush with butter. If the sheet tears during rolling, simply patch the opening with extra sheet pieces, and brush with butter.

Carefully transfer the roll to the baking tray. Bake for 10-12 minutes or until the sheet lightly browns. Remove from the oven, and transfer the roll to a cutting board.

Using a knife, cut the roll into 6-8 slices.

Serve warm.

SAUSAGE SPANAKOPITAS

serves 3 | prep time: 25 minutes | cook time: 25 minutes

Ingredients

1 tbsp. olive oil
2 garlic cloves, minced
1 small onion, peeled and diced
6 italian sausage links, chopped
1 tsp. black pepper
1 tbsp. dried oregano
salt, to taste
4 cups fresh spinach
½ cup crumbled feta cheese
1 egg
2 phyllo pastry sheets, 14x18"
2 tbsp. melted butter

Directions

Preheat the oven to 325° F.

Heat the oil in a skillet over medium. Add the onion, garlic, and sausage chunks. Sauté until the sausage is browned and cooked. Add the black pepper, oregano, and salt, and stir well. Transfer the sausage from the skillet to a medium bowl, and set aside.

With the skillet still over medium heat, add in the spinach. Sauté the spinach until wilted. Remove from the heat. Using a strainer, strain the spinach to drain any excess liquid.

Add the spinach and cheese to the sausage in a medium bowl. Fold in the egg, and mix well. Spoon the sausage mixture evenly among 4 ramekins, and set aside.

On a flat surface, lay a phyllo sheet, and lightly brush it with butter. Top the sheet with the second sheet, and cut them in half. Then cut each of the halves in half to form 4 even squares. Place 1 layered sheet on top of each ramekin, covering the sausage mixture. Using a knife, slice off the excess portions of the sheets around the ramekins' edges. Brush the tops with butter. Transfer the ramekins to the oven, and bake for 7-10 minutes or until the phyllo topping lightly browns.

Remove from the oven, and serve warm.

Perfect for a chilly romantic evening, this Latin-Caribbean soup with poached eggs will warm your mate's heart. Serve with bread for some hands-on dipping action.

SHRIMP AND SAUSAGE RICE POTTAGE

serves 2 | prep time: 25 minutes | cook time: 45 minutes

Ingredients

1 lb. shrimp, peeled and de-veined
2 tbsp. olive oil
3 garlic cloves, minced
1 large onion, peeled and diced
1 green pepper, diced
4 links chorizo sausage, chopped
½ cup fresh cilantro, chopped
3 bay leaves
1 cup seafood stock
1 cup crushed tomatoes
1 tbsp. dried oregano
½ tsp. ground coriander
½ tsp. ground annatto
1 cup jasmine rice
1 Scotch bonnet pepper, whole (optional)
6-8 cups water, hot to boiling
salt and ground black pepper, to taste
2 eggs, poached (p. 63)

Directions

Dice the shrimp into small bits, reserving 4 whole shrimp. Transfer to a bowl, and set aside.

Heat the oil in a large pot over medium. Add the garlic, onion, and green pepper. Sauté for 2-3 minutes until the garlic becomes fragrant. Stir in the sausage, cilantro, and bay leaves. Continue to sauté the ingredients for 2 additional minutes. Add the stock, crushed tomatoes, oregano, coriander, and annatto. Mix all ingredients well. Stir the rice, shrimp, scotch bonnet pepper, and 6 cups of boiling water into the pot. Season the broth with the salt and pepper to taste. Cover and allow to simmer for 35-40 minutes or until the rice cooks. Discard the bay leaves.

Serve the soup warm, topped with the poached eggs. Garnish each bowl with 1-2 whole shrimp.

Served for breakfast in many Asian countries, this Thai-inspired fried rice is loaded with breakfast favorites, like sausage, and topped with an eye-catching sunny-side up egg. Be sure to pair this dish with my lightly fried Tempura Bananas for a sweet, lasting impression.

THAI SPICY BASIL BREAKFAST FRIED RICE

serves 2 | prep time: 25 minutes | cook time: 25 minutes

Ingredients

12 shrimp, peeled and de-veined
2 tsp. ground black pepper
1 tbsp. Old Bay seasoning
1 tbsp. peanut oil
2 garlic cloves, minced
¾ cup chopped scallions
1 sweet long red pepper, diced
1½ cups fresh basil, rough chopped
3 cups cooked jasmine rice, room temperature
2 tbsp. mushroom flavored soy sauce
2-3 tbsp. oyster sauce
2 eggs, fried over easy
tomato slices for garnish

Directions

In a medium bowl, season the shrimp with the black pepper and Old Bay seasoning. Set aside.

Heat the oil in a large skillet or wok on medium-high. Stir in the garlic, scallions, and peppers. Continue to stir-fry the ingredients for 5 minutes. Stir in the shrimp and basil. Continue to stir for approximately 3-5 minutes until the shrimp begins to cook. Stir in the rice. Thoroughly mix all ingredients into the rice. Stir in the soy and oyster sauce. Mix well. Reduce the heat to medium-low. Cook for 3-5 minutes.

Serve warm, topped with the fried eggs. Garnish with tomato.

TEMPURA BANANAS

serves 2 | prep time: 10 minutes | cook time: 20 minutes

Ingredients

1 egg
1 cup water, ice cold
3 medium, well ripe bananas
1 tsp. rum extract
¾ cup flour
vegetable or peanut oil, for frying

Directions

In a medium bowl, whisk the egg and water. Stir in the rum extract. Add the flour, and mix to form a loose batter. Be sure not to overmix. Set aside.

Fill a medium skillet with the oil about halfway, and heat on medium-high.

Peel the bananas and slice diagonally into ½-inch thick pieces. Dip the banana slices into the batter, coating them. Transfer the banana slices one at a time to the oil. Fry until golden brown. Transfer to a platter lined with paper towels to drain any excess oil.

Serve warm.

INDEX